Photoshop® 7 KillerTips

Scott Kelby • Felix Nelson

WHY THIS BOOK IS AN UPDATED VERSION

"Even though Adobe comes out with a great new version of Photoshop every year or two, that doesn't mean that all the best tips on using this great program go away, to be replaced by a few hundred brand-new killer tips. We've always intended *Photoshop Killer Tips* to be the best single book on getting the most out of Photoshop, for any user. That means that a lot of the best tips from a previous version of this book will make it more or less intact into the updated version of the book. Any version-specific, relevant details get updated, of course, and we demonstrate the tips with new examples, if at all possible. And the new version of Photoshop generates plenty of brand-new killer tips, too. We want anyone picking up this book to get the best that Photoshop—and the authors—have to offer. Thanks!" .

—*SCOTT KELBY & FELIX NELSON*

PHOTOSHOP® 7 KILLER TIPS

The Photoshop® 7
Killer Tips Team

PRODUCTION AND
TECHNICAL EDITOR
Chris Main

COPY EDITOR
Barbara Thompson

PRODUCTION
Dave Damstra

COVER DESIGN AND
CREATIVE CONCEPTS
Felix Nelson

SITE DESIGN
Stacy Behan

The New Riders Team

PUBLISHER
David Dwyer

ASSOCIATE PUBLISHER
Stephanie Wall

EXECUTIVE EDITOR
Steve Weiss

MANAGING EDITOR
Kristy Knoop

PROJECT EDITOR
Suzanne Pettypiece

PROOFREADER
Linda Seifert

PUBLISHED BY
New Riders Publishing

Copyright © 2003 by Scott Kelby and the National Association of Photoshop Professionals

FIRST EDITION: August 2002

International Standard Book Number: 0-7357-1300-6

Library of Congress Catalog Card Number: 2002101873

05 04 03   7 6 5 4 3

Interpretation of the printing code: The rightmost double-digit number is the year of the book's printing; the rightmost single-digit number is the number of the book's printing. For example, the printing code 02-1 shows that the first printing of the book occurred in 2002.

Composed in Myriad and Minion by NAPP Publishing

Printed in the United States of America

Trademarks

Warning and Disclaimer

To my Dad,

Jerry Kelby,

for being

the father

everyone

wishes

they had.

—SCOTT KELBY

To Patty,

Alex, Chris,

and Earl.

They truly are

my strength

and inspiration.

—FELIX NELSON

ACKNOWLEDGMENTS

As I'm writing this acknowledgment, I'm finally learning what the downside of being a coauthor is: You only get half as much space to thank all of the great people without whom you couldn't do any of this.

First, I want to thank my incredible wife Kalebra. I don't know what she puts in her morning coffee, but it must be working. Every year she gets more amazing, more beautiful, more hilarious, more savvy, and more just plain wonderful. She's my best friend, confidant, advice desk, gourmet chef, favorite artist, and the ultimate business partner. Best of all, she's a world-class mom, and it's an absolute joy seeing her special gifts reflected in our son, Jordan. He has no idea how blessed and supremely lucky we both are to have her.

I want to thank my coauthor, Felix Nelson, for agreeing to do this book with me. He's an amazing person—a great artist, with seemingly limitless enthusiasm and energy that has him perpetually in a good mood seven days a week. His combination of talent, business savvy, and humor make him an absolute pleasure to work with, and I continue to learn more from him every day.

I want to thank my Production and Tech Editor Chris Main (two hats, no sleep) for once again bringing the whole project together and kicking butt every step of the way—even if he did sneak a few photos of his beautiful baby daughter, Kenna, into the book. Also thanks to Barbara Thompson for all her hard work and dedication to this project, and to Dave "Sporty Dave" Damstra for stepping in to "Damstrasize the pages."

I want to thank the Photoshop experts from whom I've learned so much over the years, including Julieanne Kost, Ben Willmore, Russell Preston Brown, Doug Gornick, Deke McClelland, Jack Davis, and Robb Kerr. I also want to thank my good friends and business partners, Jim Workman and Jean A. Kendra, my brother Jeff for everything he does and for being such an important part of my life. I want to thank Julie, Debbie, Kleber, Lawrence, Dave (Hey you!), Yo-Gina, Miss Ronni, Roddy, Barb, Jill, T-Bone, Pastor Dave, Rye, Stass-ee, Scotty, Melinda, Rick, Michelle, LB, Ted, and everyone at KW Media Group—they excel at the whole "David and Goliath" thing.

Thanks to Steve Weiss and David Dwyer at New Riders for their commitment to excellence, and for the honor of letting me be one of their "Voices That Matter," and to Jeff Schultz for bringing us all together.

And most importantly, an extra special thanks to God for always hearing my prayers, for always being there when I need Him, and for blessing me with a life I truly love, and a warm loving family to share it with.

—SCOTT KELBY

. . . .

First, I'd like to thank my wife Patty, who is the kindest, most understanding and caring person on the face of the planet. Her positive outlook on life, no matter how chaotic the world is around her, is remarkable. A smile from her face can light up an entire room. Then there are my three sons, Earl, Chris, and Alex. Earl is the ultimate in cool. Nothing ever ruffles his feathers. To watch this adorable, curly-headed little boy grow up into such a wonderful young man has been my greatest source of pride. And Chris "the studier" is the hardest-working, nose-to-the-grindstone person you'd ever want to meet. His drive and determination astonishes me. He's just a fantastic kid. Then there's little Alex. It's absolutely amazing how this little person affects my life. No matter how bad or how stressful the day has been, a hug from those tiny little arms and an "I love you Daddy" from those big brown eyes just melt my heart. He makes me realize things are never quite as bad as they appear.

My involvement in this book would not have been possible without the guidance and tutelage of Scott Kelby. He is without a doubt the most energetic, ambitious, and entertaining person I've ever met. His motor just never stops running. I can't begin to tell you how much he's influenced my life. He's a great mentor and a wonderful human being. I also have to thank the partners of KW Media Group (Jim Workman, Jean Kendra, and Kalebra Kelby) for the opportunities they've given me. When it comes to hard work and dedication, they're right up there with Scott. They're an amazing group and I'm a better person for knowing them.

Thanks to Dave Moser who, come hell or high water, makes sure the trains run on time. If it weren't for his efforts, this book might never had made it to the presses. Of course, I can't forget about Ted "the gameshow host" LoCascio and "Super Dave" Damstra, who do the work of ten ordinary designers. They flat out kick butt. Chris Main and Barbara Thompson could proofread an entire set of encyclopedias in an afternoon, and still have time for beer and a game of darts. I couldn't make it through the workday without them. Thanks to everyone at KW Media group, working behind the scenes, from the mailroom to customer service, who make us all look good. And a special thanks to "Rockin" Ronni, Jeff, Stacy, Scottie, and Julie. They should all be up for sainthood just for putting up with me on a daily basis.

—FELIX NELSON

Scott Kelby

Scott is Editor-in-Chief of *Photoshop User* magazine and president of the National Association of Photoshop Professionals, the trade association for Adobe® Photoshop® users. Scott is also Editor-in-Chief of *Mac Design Magazine*, a print magazine for Macintosh graphic designers, and president and CEO of KW Media Group, Inc., a Florida-based graphics training and publishing firm.

Scott is author of the books *Photoshop Down & Dirty Tricks* and *Photoshop Photo-Retouching Secrets* from New Riders Publishing, and is a contributing author to the books *Photoshop Effects Magic,* also from New Riders; *Maclopedia, the Ultimate Reference on Everything Macintosh* from Hayden Books; and *Adobe Web Design and Publishing Unleashed* from Sams.net Publishing.

Scott is an Adobe Certified Expert (ACE) in Photoshop, Training Director for the Adobe Photoshop Seminar Tour, Technical Chair for PhotoshopWorld (the convention for Adobe Photoshop users), and he is a speaker at graphics trade shows and events around the world. Scott is also featured in a series of Photoshop, Illustrator, and Web design video training tapes and has been training graphics professionals across the country since 1993.

Scott lives in the Tampa Bay area of Florida with his wife, Kalebra, and his son, Jordan. For more background info visit www.scottkelby.com.

. . . .

Felix Nelson

Felix is the Creative Director of *Photoshop User* magazine and the Senior Art Director for the National Association of Photoshop Professionals. Felix is also the Art Director for *Mac Design Magazine*.

Felix is a contributing author to the book *Photoshop Effects Magic* from New Riders Publishing and served as technical consultant for the book *Adobe Photoshop Down & Dirty Tricks*. He is also featured in a new Photoshop training video—*Photoshop Photorealistic Techniques*.

He's a traditional illustrator who took a "digital-u-turn" in 1988 when he was first introduced to a Mac IIcx. His design work and digital illustrations have been featured on NBA-, NFL-, and MLB-licensed sports apparel and have appeared in several national publications.

Felix is a guest speaker at the Adobe Photoshop Seminar Tour and is a part of the PhotoshopWorld Instructor "Dream Team."

Felix lives in Spring Hill, Florida, with his wife, Patty, and sons, Alex, Chris, and Earl.

TABLE OF CONTENTS

CHAPTER 3   56

Greased Lightnin'

Way Cool Tips

TABLE OF CONTENTS

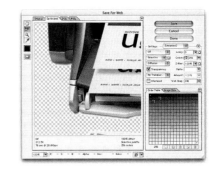

TABLE OF CONTENTS

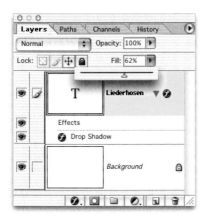

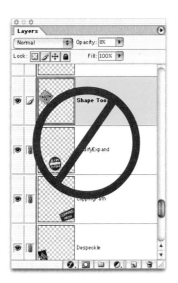

TABLE OF CONTENTS

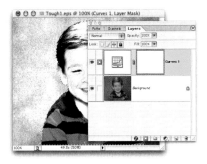

INTRODUCTION

Why we wrote this book

The inspiration for this book came when Felix saw what the car payment would be on a new Porsche Boxster. He came to me and said, "Dude, I gotta write a book." Okay, you know we're kidding, but admit it—don't you secretly wish that for once, when someone was doing something strictly for the money, they'd just come out and say so. Just once, wouldn't you like to hear someone admit it? Well, I hate to disappoint you, but I can tell you unequivocally that Felix and I absolutely did not write this book for the money. We wrote it to get free drugs. All authors get free drugs—it's in every book contract. Always has been.

Actually, the reason we wanted to write this book is because of something that is already in almost every Photoshop book ever written: the tips. You know—those cool little tips littered throughout the sidebars of all great Photoshop books. We found that those little tips were often our favorite parts of the book. In fact, Felix and I agreed that frequently we'd read all those little sidebar tips first—before we'd ever sit down to actually read a chapter. It's those neat little tips that the great authors include that make using Photoshop so much fun (and make their books so great). The only problem is, there's just not enough of 'em.

So we thought, "Wouldn't it be cool if there was a Photoshop book where the whole book, cover-to-cover, was nothing but those little tips on the side!" Then Felix jumped up and yelled, "Let's write that book!" I jumped up and yelled, "Yes, yes! We have to write that book. It's our destiny!" Then Felix yelled, "Then I can get my Porsche!" I mean, he yelled, "This book will help humanity and be written for the common good" (or something like that. I can't remember. Probably because of all the drugs).

Is this book for you?

Is this book for you? Are you kidding? This book is *so* for you that it secretly freaks you out. Look, we don't know you personally, but we know Photoshop people. You're just like us—you love those little sidebar tips just as much as we do. If you didn't, authors would've stopped adding them to their books years ago, because, frankly, they're a pain in the butt to compile. But we know what you're thinking. Sure, you love those little tips—those inside secrets that make you look smart at parties and gain respect from your peers, homies, peeps, and other esteemed colleagues, but you want something more. You want the one thing that those cool little sidebar tips never seem to have. That's right, graphics. As cool as those sidebar tips are, they're always just a tiny little box with a couple of lines of text (like the sidebar we added above left). So we thought we'd expand the explanations just enough to make them more accessible, and add an accompanying graphic to enhance each tip's innate juiciness. They must remain "juicy." They must be "juicy tips."

Now you're probably wondering, "Guys, Photoshop is one amazing program with an unrivaled power and incredible depth. Couldn't you have come up with at least 1,000 Photoshop tips?" Absolutely. We could have included loads of tips, such as "F7 brings up the Layers palette," and "Press Shift-G to get the Paint Bucket tool," but the problem is, those aren't "Killer Tips." Every Photoshop book has those tips. Heck, books about gardening probably even have those Photoshop tips. For a tip to get in this book, it had to be a "Killer Tip." Each tip had to be one that would make the reader smile, nod, and then pick up the phone to call another Photoshop user just to "tune them up" with their newfound power. Remember, these are killer tips, so be careful. Someone could get hurt.

Okay, how do I get started?

In both of my previous Photoshop books, *Photoshop 7 Down & Dirty Tricks* and *Photoshop 6 Photo-Retouching Secrets,* I used a technique that really worked well. I gratuitously mentioned both of my other books in the introduction, just in case I didn't get to plug them later. No, wait… that's not it. What I *did* tell the reader was that my books aren't set up like a novel. They're purposely not designed to make you start at Chapter One and read your way through to the back (where hopefully, I'll again have an opportunity to plug, I mean casually mention, my other books). Instead, this book is designed so you can jump in anywhere, in any chapter, and immediately try the tips that interest you the most, regardless of your level of experience in Photoshop. You don't need to load any special images from a CD-ROM or go to a Web site to download special photos—these are just cool tips. No flaming type, no multilevel glows—just timesaving shortcuts and efficiency tips that will make you faster and better at Photoshop than you'd ever thought you'd be.

Also, like my previous books, we spell out everything. So if you've been using Photoshop for years, don't let it frustrate you because instead of just writing, "Create a new layer," we usually write, "Create a new layer by clicking on the New Layer icon at the bottom of the Layers palette." We do that because we want everyone, at any skill level, to be able to open the book to any page and start applying these cool tips to their work immediately.

This book is built on the premise that "Speed Kills." Because after all, if you get faster at Photoshop, you'll have more time to be creative, and the more time you spend being creative, the more fun you'll have.

Is this book for Macintosh, Windows, or both?

This book is not only for Mac and Windows users, it's for people who don't even have a computer. In fact, it's ideal for anyone with $39.99 (kidding). Because Photoshop is identical on both the Macintosh and Windows operating systems, the book is for both Mac and Windows users. However, the keyboards on a Mac and PC are slightly different, so every time we give a keyboard shortcut, we give both the Mac and Windows shortcuts. (Well, there is one other difference— in Mac OS X you'll find Photoshop's Preferences under the new Photoshop menu instead of the Edit menu like it used to be in the Mac OS and still is in Windows).

How to use this book

This book is designed to be read while moving at a high rate of speed. If you're barreling down the highway going 80 mph, weaving in and out of traffic, that's the ideal time to turn to Chapter 6 to read the tip on "How to assist EMS workers with using the Jaws of Life." Okay, admittedly, that's probably not a good idea, so instead, just make sure you open this book in front of your computer so you can dive right into the tips. Remember, the one who dies with the most cool tips wins.

What not to do

You're almost ready to get to the tips, but first a word of caution: "Caution." There. Now you're ready. Actually, we did want to point out that the only two actual sidebar tips in the entire book are in the sidebars on these two pages. So, don't go rippin' through the book looking for all those little sidebar tips because we intentionally left the sidebars blank. Why? So we could write another book called *The Missing Killer Tips Sidebars,* just in case Felix ever sees what the payment is for a house on the beach.

TIP

You're doing it again! Stop looking at these sidebars. See, they're intoxicating—you're drawn to them even after you know it's not really a tip. Okay, here's a real tip: If you like sidebar tips, buy this book.

Life in the Fast Lane

PRODUCTION TIPS

Imagine a pig. Wait, not the sloppy grunting kind. Imagine that cute pig from the movie Babe. *Clean, well-kempt, with a broad vocabulary and a slightly*

Life in the Fast Lane
production tips

British accent. Ahh, that's better. Now, imagine that he somehow stumbled into a giant vat of grease, jumped out, and began to run at full speed. If you decided to try and catch him with your bare hands (and it's a reasonable assumption that you would), how easy would that be?

Now, think of this chapter as "the making of the pig." But now you're the pig, and your competition is trying to catch you. But after learning the tips in this chapter, you're "faster than a greased pig" in Photoshop. Okay, I admit this whole pig thing isn't the greatest metaphor. Let's try this. You're an eagle; a soaring proud bird. And you've somehow fallen into a giant vat of grease. Suddenly, a shot rings out.... I'm not sure I like where this is going.

Let's try this: Every day you spend time in Photoshop. Some of it is fun, creative time. Some of it is boring production time, such as making selections, loading brush sets, applying Curves, cropping, transforming—you know, boring stuff. But if you could greatly speed up the boring stuff, that would leave more time for the fun, creative stuff, right? When you strip away all the greased-pig metaphors, that's what this chapter is really about. Run, Babe, run!

BRUSHES RIGHT WHERE YOU WANT 'EM

When Photoshop 6 shipped, a lot of people freaked out because the floating Brushes palette—the one they loved and cherished more than they realized—was gone. It was replaced by a Brush Picker that was docked to the Options Bar up top.

Fortunately, not only is the Brushes palette back in Photoshop 7.0 but it also comes with a much more powerful Brush Engine. But here's a tip that gives you something faster and more convenient for switching to another preset brush than using the Brushes palette—and you might find that you like it even better. Just press the Control key, then click within your image (PC: Right-click) and the Brush Picker will appear directly under your cursor. Plus, in 7.0 you can even change the Master Diameter of the brush that you choose in the Picker. This is one you'll have to try to appreciate the sheer speed and convenience of putting your brushes at your fingertips anytime.

CHANGE A BRUSH HERE—IT SHOWS UP THERE

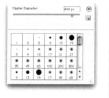
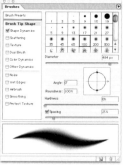

Okay, in Photoshop 7.0, there's still the Brush Picker (up in the Options Bar), and there's also the floating Brushes palette from the Window menu. If you want to create a new custom brush, where should you do it? Luckily, it doesn't matter—any changes you make in the floating Brushes palette will automatically be reflected in the Brush Picker. It's like an evil clone, without all the evil.

⬤ ⬤ ⬤ NO MORE JAGGY LASSO TOOL SELECTIONS

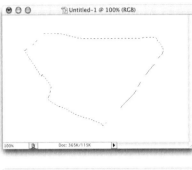

Have you ever tried to create a smooth selection using the Lasso tool? It's just about impossible, right? (If it sounds like it isn't, give it a try—open a new document, take the Lasso tool, and draw any random selection, and then look at the selection. It's jaggy—not crazy jaggy, but it's certainly not smooth.) If you were trying to create a selection for an interface design, or a realistic element of some sort, it would just be too jaggy to use. Here's a tip:

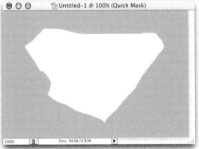

(1) Draw the area you want to use as your selection with the Lasso tool.

(2) Press the letter "q" to enter Quick Mask mode (your selection will now be surrounded by solid pink).

(3) Go under the Filter menu, under Noise, and choose Median. As you raise the Radius of the Median filter, you'll see your edges smooth out.

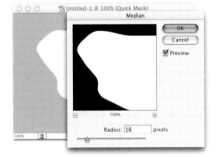

(4) When it looks nice and smooth, press the letter "q" again to return to Standard mode, and you'll have nothing but a nice smooth selection.

Look at the selection in the first image above. See how those jaggies have been replaced by the smooth edges—courtesy of the Median filter?

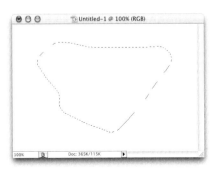

LET PHOTOSHOP DO THE WORK IN CURVES

Let's say you're using the Curves dialog box for correcting images and you have an image where you're trying to adjust the color of some green plants. How do you know where that particular green "lives" on the curve so you can dial in and adjust it? Photoshop can tell you—in fact, you can have Photoshop automatically plot that color on the curve for you. With the Curves dialog open, just Command-click (PC: Control-click) on that color within your image. Photoshop will then add a point to the curve that represents the spot you sampled, and now you're ready to tweak it.

WANT A FINER GRID? YOU GOT IT!

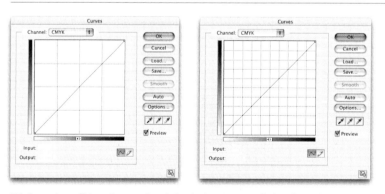

While we're talking Curves, by default the Curves dialog box displays a 25% grid (shown above left). If you'd like a finer grid, you can Option-click (PC: Alt-click) once within the grid, and it will then display a 10% grid (shown above right).

YOU DON'T NEED THE BRUSHES PALETTE TO CHANGE BRUSH SIZE

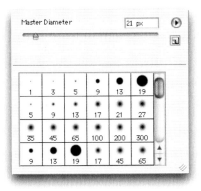

Adobe has been tweaking the shortcuts for changing your brush sizes via the keyboard. In older versions of Photoshop, you could move to the next largest brush in the palette by pressing the Right Bracket key (]), and the next smallest by pressing the Left Bracket key ([). In Photoshop 6.0.1 and 7.0, however, pressing those keys increases/decreases the size of your brush by 10 pixels each time you press them. Once your brush goes over 100 pixels in size, it then moves in 25-pixel increments, and if you go over 200 pixels it moves in 50-pixel increments.

ROTATE TO ANY ANGLE THE FAST WAY

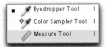

If you have a specific angle that you'd like to rotate a layer to, it's easy. Get the Measure tool (it looks like a ruler and is in the Eyedropper tool's flyout menu in the Toolbox), and click-and-drag out a line at the desired angle. Then go under the Edit menu, under Transform, and choose Rotate. Your layer will instantly rotate to match the angle that you drew with the Measure tool. (Note: To rotate an entire layer, you must select it first [Command-A for Mac, Control-A for PC].)

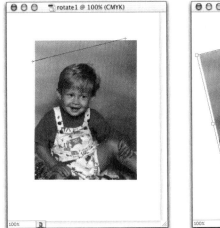

DON'T STOP ZOOMING JUST BECAUSE YOU'RE CORRECTING

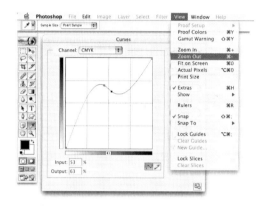

If you're in the Curves or Levels dialog box and you want to view your image at a different magnification, don't worry. Even though most of Photoshop's menus are grayed out and unaccessible, the View menu is still active, and you can choose different views from there (as shown at left), or you can still use the standard navigation keyboard shortcuts. Try it yourself: Open Levels or Curves and then press Command-+ (PC: Control-+) or Command-minus sign (PC: Control-minus sign) to zoom in or out. You can also hold the Spacebar (which temporarily switches you to the Hand tool) and navigate around your image. If you forgot to open the Info palette (or any other palette for that matter), you can still access it by choosing it from the Window menu.

INSTANTLY FIND THE CENTER OF ANY OBJECT

This is a great tip for quickly finding the exact center of any object on a layer. You start by pressing Command-T (PC: Control-T) to bring up the Free Transform bounding box. The bounding box has a handle in the center of both sides and center handles at both the top and bottom. Now all you have to do is make Photoshop's rulers visible (Command-R on Mac, Control-R on PC), and then drag out a horizontal and a vertical ruler guide to these handles to mark the center.

NEW DOCUMENT SIZES—HAVE IT YOUR WAY

Do you wind up using the same size, color mode, and resolution a lot when creating new documents? For example, let's say that you're a Web designer and you design a lot of standard-size Web banners. Ideally, every time you open a new image, it would be 468x60 pixels, at 72 ppi in RGB mode, but the problem is that every time you copy a selection, Photoshop automatically uses the data from that last copied selection and enters it into the New dialog box for you, thinking you want to "paste your selection in." It's a great convenience if that's what you wanted it to do; a great annoyance if you didn't. So here's how to have Photoshop create your ideal-sized document any time you want by pressing just one button:

	New Action	
Name:	New image 468x60	Record
Set:	Default Actions.atn	Cancel
Function Key:	F5 ☐ Shift ☐ Command	
Color:	☐None	

(1) Go under the Window menu and choose Show Actions. Click the New Action icon at the bottom of the Actions palette (it's the second from the right), and when the New Action dialog box appears, name your action (we chose "New image 468x60"), and then assign this action to an open F-key on your keyboard by choosing it from the pop-up menu.

(2) Next, click the Record button, and then go to the File menu and choose New. Enter your desired default size, unit of measurement, resolution, and color mode, and click OK. Then return to the Actions palette and click the Stop button at the bottom of the palette (it's the first icon from the left).

Actions
Move current layer
Merge Layers
Save
Close
Close
Open
Save
New image 468x60

You did it—you just created your own custom default image size. Now, let's test it—press the F-key on your keyboard that you chose earlier, and a new document will instantly appear with your own custom settings already in place. You can assign other actions to other commonly used sizes. You'll be amazed at how much time and frustration this one tip can save. Pretty sweet!

GET RID OF UNWANTED BRUSHES

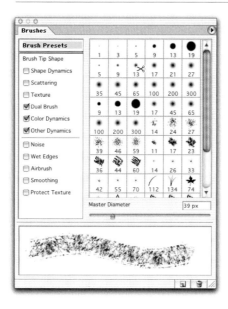

You probably already know that you can add a brush to the Brushes palette, but did you know that it's even easier to delete them? Just hold the Option key (PC: Alt key) and you'll notice that your cursor changes into a pair of scissors (as shown at left on the 13-pixel, soft-edged brush). Click once on the brush you want to delete and that baby's gone—no warning dialog, no chance to change your mind—it's gone.

NAVIGATING THE BRUSH PICKER LIKE A PRO

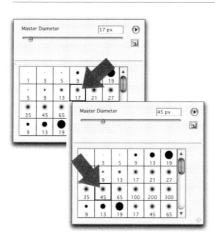

Now that you've learned how to bring up the Brush Picker right where you want it, it wouldn't hurt to learn this quick navigation tip to keep you from spending more time there than is necessary. Once you've selected a brush in the Picker, just use the Arrow keys on your keyboard to navigate up, down, left, or right to other brushes. Once you choose a brush and you are no longer in the Brush Picker, you can use the Period and Comma keys to move forward and backward through the different brushes. Shift-period and Shift-comma will jump you to the first and last brushes in the Brushes palette, respectively.

⬤ ⬤ ⬤ GET MORE CONTROL OVER YOUR PAINT STROKES

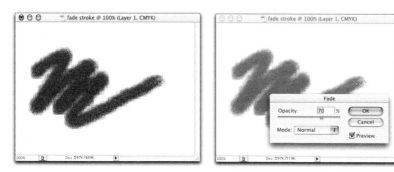

Photoshop lets you affect a brush stroke even after you've painted it using Photoshop's Fade Brush Tool command (found under the Edit menu). Fade works like "undo on a slider," and dragging the Opacity slider all the way to the left will completely undo your freshly painted brush stroke, but if you stop anywhere before the far left side, it will instead give you a percentage of undo, lightening your stroke. You can also use the pop-up Mode menu to alter how your stroke blends with the object below it.

⬤ ⬤ ⬤ SPEED TIP TO ROTATE THROUGH OPEN IMAGES

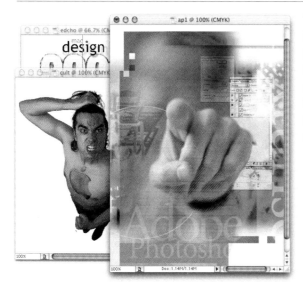

This tip (Right-click-Tab) has been in the Windows version of Photoshop for quite some time, but since Photoshop 6.0 Macintosh users can do it too—press Control-Tab to move from one open image to the next, rotating through to any of your open windows.

CHAPTER 1 • Production Tips   11

HIDING THOSE ANNOYING MARCHING ANTS

Anytime you make a selection (with the Lasso tool, Magic Wand, etc.), the edges of your selection blink on and off to indicate the border of your selected area. Because these edges appear to be moving, they gained the nickname "marching ants" (because that's pretty much what they look like—a row of marching ants). These "marching ants" can often be distracting if you're trying to edit or retouch an image, but you can hide them from view by pressing Command-H (PC: Control-H), which is the shortcut for "Show/Hide Extras." This is an incredibly handy feature because your selection is still active, but the annoying "marching ants" aren't visible. The only downside is that, after you've made your adjustments, you have to remember to make the marching ants visible again by pressing Command-H (PC: Control-H).

MAKING YOUR GUIDE FLIP

Just like most page-layout applications, Photoshop has non-printing guides you can pull out anytime you need to align objects (or type as shown at left), but there's also a trick for flipping the guides. To access the guides, make your rulers visible by pressing Command-R (PC: Control-R), then click-and-hold within one of the rulers and drag out a guide. If you pull out a horizontal guide from the top ruler, but really wanted a vertical guide, just press the Option key (PC: Alt key) and your guide will flip from horizontal to vertical (pretty slick). You can pull out as many guides as you need (there's probably a limit to how many you can use, but we've never reached it). When you're done using a guide, just drag it back to the ruler where it came from. To remove all of your guides at once, choose Clear Guides from the View menu.

CREATING TEMPORARY BRUSHES

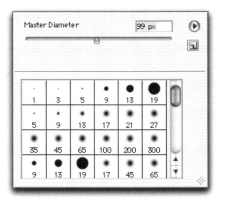

It's easy to create a temporary brush based on your preset brushes in Photoshop 7.0. Just click on the Brush Sample in the Options Bar to bring up the Brushes Picker. With the Master Diameter slider you can change your brush size from 1 to 2500 pixels. If you like the size of your new brush and you want to save it, just click the New Brush icon at the top right of the dialog. The Brush Name dialog will appear so you can name your new brush. When you click OK, the new brush will immediately be added to your Brushes palette.

REUSING YOUR LAST CURVE SETTING

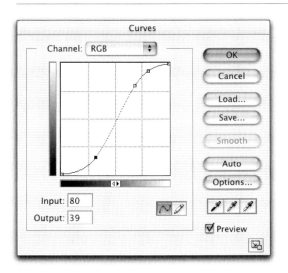

Once you've applied a curve setting to an image, it's very possible that you'd like to use that exact same setting again, or maybe you'd just like to tweak that setting a bit. Well, you can. To bring up the Curves dialog with the last curve you used still in place, press Option-Command-M (PC: Alt-Control-M).

BRINGING BACK THOSE CROPPED AWAY AREAS

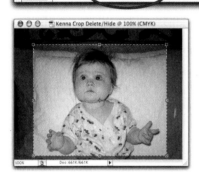

When you're using the Crop tool to crop images, you'll find that you actually have some options on how the area you're cropping is handled after the crop. For example, in the Options Bar (as long as you're not on the Background layer) you'll see an option that lets you either Delete the cropped areas or simply Hide them from view (in other words, the areas are still there, they just expand into the Canvas area). If you choose the Hide option, it crops the image window down to the size of the crop, but since the cropped-away areas are still really there, you can use the Move tool to drag these cropped areas back into view.

FIX THOSE STRAY PIXELS FAST!

Sometimes when making a selection with the Magic Wand tool or Color Range (under the Select menu), Photoshop will leave little stray pixels unselected. You can tell where they are because they appear to twinkle on and off, kind of teasing...nay, taunting you, because your selection is not complete. Luckily, there's a quick way to rein in those renegade stray pixels. Go under the Select menu, under Modify, and choose Smooth. Enter a Sample Radius of 1 pixel and click OK. That will usually do the trick—those stray pixels are now selected.

GETTING MORE CONTROL OVER THE MAGIC WAND

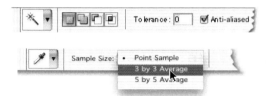

By default, the Eyedropper tool's Sample Size option (in the Options Bar) is set to "Point Sample," which comes into play if you're using it to read values for color correction. But for now, it's important to know that the Sample Size option chosen for the Eyedropper tool actually affects how the Magic Wand tool makes its selection (the two have an undocumented relationship). If you increase the Eyedropper's Sample Size to 3 by 3 or 5 by 5 Average, the Magic Wand will select an average of a much larger range of pixels in the sample area. This is important to know, because if you don't have Point Sample chosen and you set the Magic Wand Tolerance to 0, it won't just select the individual pixel you click on—it will select all of the pixels that match any of the pixels in the sample. The next time your Magic Wand isn't behaving the way it used to, check and see if you have changed the Eyedropper tool Sample Size.

MAKING THE COLOR PALETTE WORK TWICE AS HARD

If you use the Color palette to select colors, you're probably already using the color ramp at the bottom of the palette for making quick color selections, but here are two tips that make using the ramp faster and easier. First, the color ramp doesn't have to use the same color mode as the color sliders above it; for example, you can have RGB for your sliders and grayscale as your ramp. This is great because it gives you two different models to choose from without digging through menus. You can choose the color modes for both the sliders and the ramp from the Color palette's pop-down menu. The second tip is that if you quickly want to change color ramps, Shift-click on the ramp. Every time you click, it will rotate through to the next color mode.

NEW DOCUMENT TIMESAVER

This is a *huge* timesaver, and once you start using it, you'll use it almost every day. It enables you to create a new document that automatically matches the exact dimensions, color mode, and resolution of any other document that you already have open. Here's how: Go under the File menu and choose New. When the New document dialog box opens, go under the Window menu, under Documents, and you'll see a list of all your open documents at the bottom of the menu. Choose the document you want to emulate, and its size, color mode, and resolution will instantly be entered into your New document dialog box—all you have to do is click OK, and a new document with those specs will appear. This one may sound a bit lightweight, until you try it a couple of times.

REARRANGING YOUR BRUSHES

One of the things in Photoshop that just didn't make sense to us was that you couldn't easily rearrange the order of your brushes in the Brushes palette. Oh sure, you could create a whole new custom set with the brushes you wanted, in the order you wanted them, but it would take a while, and frankly, was such a pain that we only know a handful of people that actually went through the trouble. Well, our wish for easily rearranging brushes is finally here, but the process is a bit hidden beneath the surface. To move a brush from one spot in the palette to another, go under the Edit menu, and choose Preset Manager. In the Preset Manager dialog, under Preset Type, choose Brushes. Then, hold the Command key (PC: Control key) and you can click-and-drag the brush of your choice to the location of your choice. At last, we are free to move brushes among the herd.

USE YOUR LAST SETTINGS AND SAVE TIME

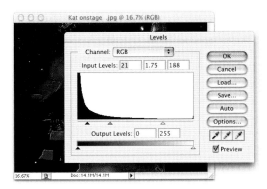

This is a tip that will save you time when you're making tonal adjustments using Levels, Curves, Color Balance, etc. (most anything that appears under the Adjustments menu under the Image menu). When you bring up one of the tonal adjustment dialogs, it always displays its default settings, but if you hold the Option key (PC: Alt key) when choosing it from the Adjustments menu, instead of coming up with the default settings, it will display the last settings you used in that particular dialog box. You can also add the Option (PC: Alt) key to keyboard shortcuts. For example, the shortcut to bring up the Levels dialog box is Command-L (PC: Control-L), but if you add Option (PC: Alt) to those keys, the Levels dialog box will open with your last-used settings.

HIT THOSE CHANNELS FAST

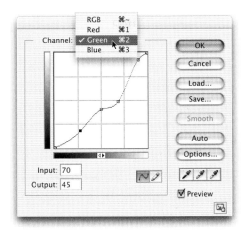

When you're in the Curves dialog, if you're charging by the hour, you can certainly travel up to the Channel pop-up menu and choose each individual channel you want to work on, but if you want to do it the fast way, just press Command-1 for Red, Command-2 for Green, and Command-3 for Blue (PC: Control-1, Control-2, etc.). If you need to return to the composite RGB channel, press Command-Tilde (PC: Control-Tilde). By the way, the Tilde key looks like ~, and it lives right above the Tab key on your keyboard. Don't feel bad. Nobody knows what the Tilde key is. We're not sure it's a real symbol at all. We think it was made up so there wouldn't be an empty space there on your keyboard. Hey, it's somewhat plausible.

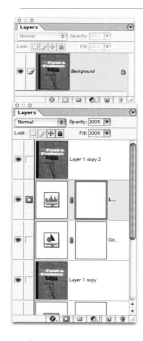

HOW TO GET AN UNDO AFTER YOU'VE CLOSED THE DOCUMENT

As you probably already know, the History palette keeps track of the last 20 changes to your document that you can use for multiple undos when working on a project. The only bad part is that when you close your document, your undos (in History) are automatically deleted. However, there is a way to save an undo, as long as it's a tonal adjustment (such as Curves, Levels, Color Balance, etc.), by creating Adjustment layers. Just click on the half-white, half-black circle at the bottom of the Layers palette and choose your tonal adjustment from the pop-up to create an Adjustment layer. These Adjustment layers are saved as layers, along with your file. That way, the next time you open the file, you can go back and edit your Curves, Levels, etc. adjustment by double-clicking on the Adjustment layer. The last applied adjustment will appear, and you can edit it live. If you decide you don't want the original adjustment applied at all, you can drag the Adjustment layer into the Trash icon at the bottom of the Layers palette. You can also add a Gradient Fill, a Pattern Fill, and even a Solid Color fill as an Adjustment layer, giving you an undo at a later date, because again, they're saved as layers with the file.

USING THE PEN? STAY AWAY FROM THE TOOLBOX

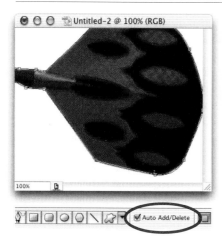

Want to save trips to the Toolbox when using the Pen tool? You're in luck. Better yet, you don't even have to hold down any modifier keys (such as Option/Alt, etc.), because Photoshop will do the work for you. Here's why: When you draw a path, move your cursor over a line segment, and your Pen cursor automatically changes to the Add Anchor Point tool so you can click anywhere along that path to add a point. Move your cursor over an existing point, and it changes into the Delete Anchor Point tool (click on the point, and it's deleted). This is called "Auto Add/Delete," and it's on by default (you can turn if off, should you want to, using the checkbox in the Options Bar).

PUT YOUR GRADIENT PICKER AT YOUR FINGERTIPS

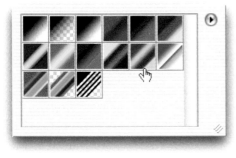

Remember the very first tip in this chapter—how to make the Brush Picker appear under your cursor in your image window? Well, it doesn't just stop with the Brush Picker. You can pull the same stunt with the Gradient Picker as well, and have access to your gradient library by Control-clicking within your image area (PC: Right-click). It also works with the Custom Shape Picker. Here's an even slicker trick: You can use the Return or Enter key instead to bring up the Gradient or Custom Shape Pickers.

DON'T CLICK IN THAT FIELD!

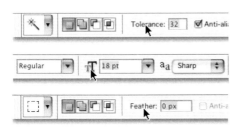

Those tiny little fields up in the Options Bar can really be a pain sometimes, especially if you're trying to highlight a field, delete the current value, and type in a new one. Instead of doing all that, just click on the field's name and Photoshop will automatically highlight the entire field for you. That way, you can just type in new values and it will automatically replace the old values. Great thing is, this doesn't just work in the Options Bar; it works in many of Photoshop's palettes, including the Character and Paragraph palettes.

⚫ ⚫ ⚫ OUT OF MEMORY? TRY THIS FIRST

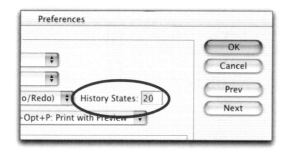

Here's a tip for avoiding those nasty out-of-memory warning dialogs. One of the reasons Photoshop needs so much memory is that by default it keeps a snapshot of the last 20 things you did to your document, thus allowing you to undo your previous 20 steps. (You can see the running list of your last 20 steps in the History palette.) As you might expect, storing 20 steps takes a mighty chunk of memory, and if you're running a little low (or getting those evil out-of-memory warnings), one thing you might try is lowering the amount of steps Photoshop stores. In Mac OS X, go under the Photoshop menu, under Preferences, under General, and you'll find a field for History States. (In Windows and Mac OS 9.x, you'll find Preferences under the Edit menu.) You can lower this number (try 8 States for starters), and you may avoid the dreaded memory warnings. Just remember, by lowering the States, you don't have 20 undos anymore.

⚫ ⚫ ⚫ HOW TO "UNERASE"

You probably already know that you can use the History Brush as an "undo" on a brush, and that by default, the History Brush paints back to how your image looked when you first opened it. But did you know that the Eraser tool has a similar function? That's right, the next time you've got the Eraser tool chosen, look up in the Options Bar and you'll see a checkbox for "Erase to History." Normally, the Eraser tool erases to your Background color, but when you turn on this checkbox, it erases back to what the image looked like when you opened it.

OPEN UP SOME SCREEN REAL ESTATE

A lot of times when you're working on a project, your screen can get really cluttered with palettes (Photoshop is an especially palette-heavy application). If you want all the palettes out of the way for your convenience while you're working, just press Shift-Tab to hide them, or Shift-Tab to bring them back. The Menu Bar, the Options Bar, and the Toolbox will all still be visible.

COPY ONE LAYER, OR COPY 'EM ALL

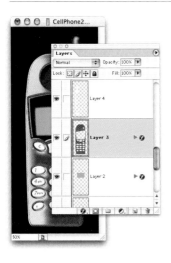

If you're working on a layered document and you make a selection and copy that selection, by default Photoshop only copies the information on your currently active layer (and that's a good thing). However, there may be times when you want to copy your selection as if the image was flattened (in other words, you want to copy everything on all visible layers). If that's the case, press Shift-Command-C (PC: Shift-Control-C), and you'll copy as if the image was flattened, not just on the active layer.

STUCK IN A FIELD? HERE'S HOW TO ESCAPE

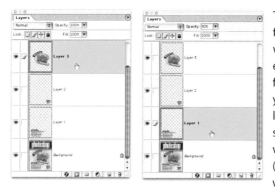

This is one of those tips that keeps you from pulling your hair out. Sometimes when you're editing values in a field (for example, you're typing in Opacity numbers for a layer) and you've entered the number you want, Photoshop doesn't let you leave that field (meaning your cursor is still flashing in the Opacity field). It gets worse if you've switched to any other layer (besides the Background layer) and you want to use a keyboard shortcut to switch tools. For example, you press the letter "t" to switch to the Type tool, but instead of getting the Type tool, you get an error "bong" because your cursor is still in the Opacity field and you can't type letters in a number field. Here's how to get around it. Just press the Return (Enter) key on your keyboard to lock in the change in your field and release your keyboard for other tasks.

DON'T CANCEL; RESET AND SAVE TIME

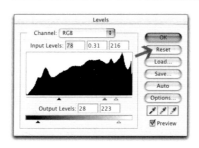

Most of Photoshop's dialog boxes (but not all) will let you use this little tip, which can save you loads of time. When you're making changes in a dialog box (let's use the Levels dialog box as an example) and decide that you don't like the changes you've made, you can press the Cancel button to close the dialog box, leaving your image unchanged. Then you can reopen the dialog and try again. This is an incredible waste of valuable time, so instead, Photoshop lets you "reset" the dialog—putting the settings back to what they were when you first opened it. Just hold the Option key (PC: Alt key) and look at the Cancel button—it changes into the Reset button. Click it, and it resets the dialog automatically, as if you hadn't made any changes at all. Big, big timesaver.

TIME FOR SOME PANTONE CONVENIENCE

If you're using Pantone colors often in your work, you'll kill a lot of time if you pick your colors by clicking on the Color Swatches in the Toolbox to bring up the Color Picker, and then click on the Custom button to bring up the Custom Color Picker where you can type in the number of the Pantone color you want (if you're lucky enough to know that number off the top of your head. If not, then you'll have to scroll through the Pantone Color Picker). But there's a faster, easier way—load the Pantone colors into your Swatches palette. You do that by opening the Swatches palette (found under the Window menu), and in the palette's pop-down menu, choose Pantone Solid Coated. A dialog will appear asking whether you want to add (Append) these Pantone colors to your existing swatches or replace the current swatches with the Pantone set (I'd choose replace, but hey, that's just me). Then, in the palette's pop-down menu, choose Small List to display both a swatch and the color's Pantone number.

CHANGE VALUES EVEN FASTER BY USING YOUR KEYBOARD

Here's another timesaver when you're entering values into fields (and you wind up doing this quite a bit, so anything you can do to save time here is a blessing). When you've highlighted a field, you can use the Up/Down Arrow keys on your keyboard to raise/lower the value. If you add the Shift key (Shift-Up/Down Arrow), it raises/lowers the value in larger increments. For example, if you're creating type and you highlight the Font Size field, pressing the Up Arrow key raises the point size by 1 point each time you press it. Using Shift-Up Arrow raises the point size by 10 points each time you press it.

TOGGLING ON THE TOOLBOX

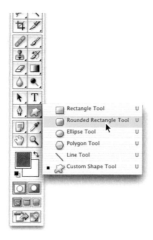

Many of the tools in Photoshop's Toolbox have additional tools in flyout menus that appear when you click on a tool and hold for a moment, but there's actually a faster way to select tools than waiting for the list to appear—just Option-click (PC: Alt-click) on the tool and each time you do, one of the other tools from the flyout menu will come to the front. Just stop when the one you want appears. (Note: The tools that have this "flyout menu" have a tiny black, right-facing triangle in the lower right-hand corner of the tool.)

USE THE MOVE TOOL ANYTIME

When you're using just about any of Photoshop's tools, you can temporarily switch to the Move tool at any time by simply holding the Command key (PC: Control key). It's temporary, and as soon as you release it, you're back to the tool you started with.

PHOTOSHOP REMEMBERS THE LAST SIZE YOU INPUT

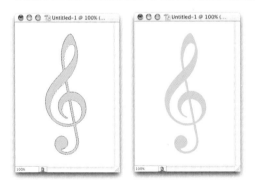

Although there's no way to set a default size for your New document dialog box (outside of creating an action to do it for you), there's a pretty cool little-known tip that lets you open a new document using the last settings you manually input. Just press Option-Command-N (PC: Alt-Control-N) and the New document dialog will appear using the last settings you input (rather than using the clipboard data to determine the new document size).

HOW TO HIDE THE PATH AROUND YOUR SHAPE

When you're using the Shape tool, by default it creates a Shape layer (and there are a number of reasons why you might want that) with a path around the shape. Most of the time, you don't need to see the path border around your shape (unless, of course, you want to edit that border), so to hide it from view, press Shift-Command-H (PC: Shift-Control-H).

REMOVING POINTS FROM THE POLYGONAL LASSO

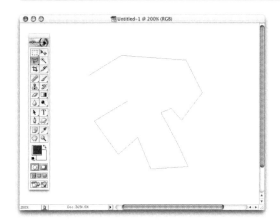

When you're using the Polygonal Lasso tool, every time you click to change directions, it automatically lays down a point where you pivoted. If you added a point and didn't mean to, you can delete it by pressing the Delete (PC: Backspace) key. Every time you press Delete (PC: Backspace), it deletes another previous point (in the order they were created). In fact, if you really mess up, you can keep pressing Delete until you're right back where you started.

FIND THE CENTER OF ANY DOCUMENT

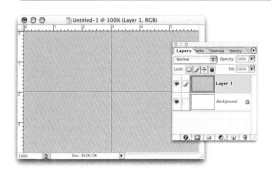

Need to find the exact center of your image? All you need is a layer filled with your Foreground color, and Photoshop will do the rest (okay, you have to do a little, but Photoshop will certainly help). First, create a new layer and fill it with your Foreground color. Make your rulers visible and drag a guide down from the top ruler. It will automatically snap to the exact horizontal center of your image. Do the same with the side ruler, and it automatically snaps to the vertical center of your image. (Note: if there's not any snapping going on, make sure that Snap is turned on under the View menu.)

BUT I WANTED THE OLD BRUSHES PALETTE BACK

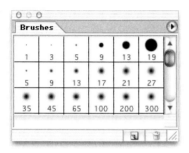

I know, I know, you opened Photoshop 7.0's Brushes palette, hoping it would look like the one you used back in Photoshop 4.0/5.0/5.5, but instead, it's this huge mega palette. If you wish it were just that convenient, tiny palette from days gone by, fear not—it's only a few clicks away. Just bring up the Brushes palette, and from the palette's pop-down menu, choose Expanded View (which is on by default). All the scary looking sliders will go away, leaving you with the tiny palette you long for. If it doesn't look "just" like the old one, make sure Small Thumbnail is selected from the palette's pop-down menu, and if the palette is stretched too wide, just drag in the corner and you're back in business. You can even use the old F5 Function key keyboard shortcut, like the days of old (life was simpler then).

SEEING YOUR CURVES UP CLOSE

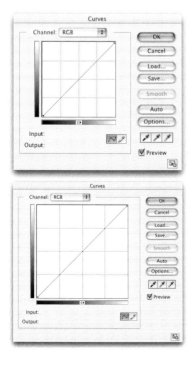

For some weird reason, the trendy thing to do now is to use a monitor display setting that makes your icons so small, it's really just about a blind guess as to which program or file you're clicking (or double-clicking) on. This becomes more of a problem when you're doing a Curves adjustment, because the dialog box that once looked so huge at 640x480 pixels, now looks tiny at 1280x960. But fear not, Adobe added a tiny, innocent-looking button at the bottom right-hand corner of the Curves dialog box, and when you click on it, it gives you a significantly larger version of Curves so you can finally see what you're doing. By the way, if your menus are so small you can't read them, this will help—the keyboard shortcut for Curves is Command-M (PC: Control-M). Sorry, that last part was sass. Total sass. Mega-sass. I feel really bad about it.

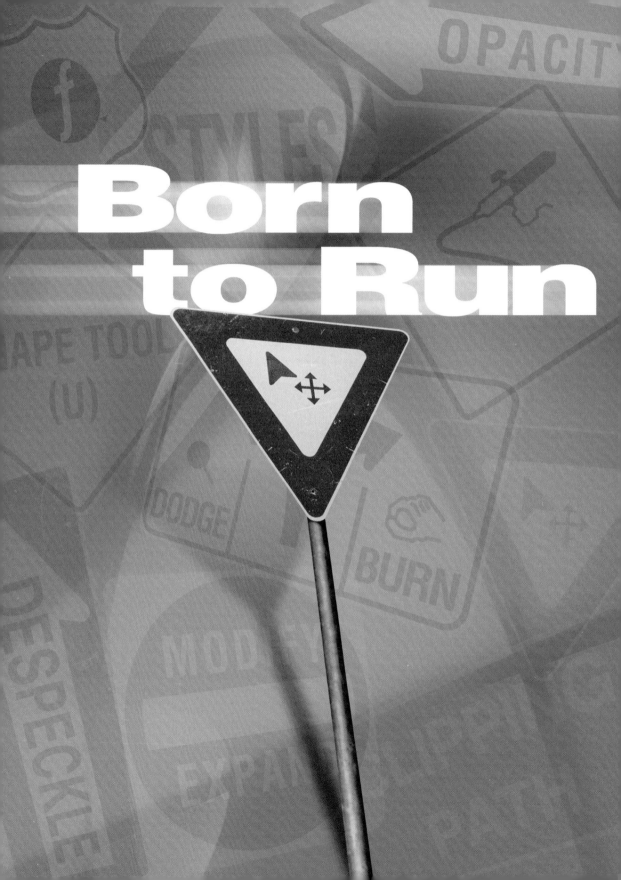

Have you ever been to one of those trendy Photoshop parties? You know the ones I mean—where the guests sit around in the study, ensconced in

Born to Run

essential tips you've got to know

big leather chairs, smoking smuggled Cuban cigars, and casually chatting about "calculating this, and masking that…," and they keep referring to the time they were out on their yacht with Deke, Ben, and Jack. Don't you hate those parties? Me too. But nonetheless, I don't want to get caught at one of them and be the only goober there who didn't know that Shift-Delete is the undocumented shortcut for bringing up the Fill dialog box. Imagine the shame. Then you'd have to pull that old, "Oh, I knew that, I thought you were referring to something in the Curves dialog that I heard at RIT," as they all slowly look away, rolling their eyes, glancing at each other with that "who's the spaz?" look on their faces. Do you want to be that person. Do you want to be that spaz? No? Then read this chapter, dammit. Memorize every word, every line, every keyboard shortcut. Then fire up a fat boy and head for the study. It's time to find a spaz to tease until he's in the fetal position.

USING THE LASSO TOOL? KEEP IT STRAIGHT

We normally use the Lasso tool for drawing freeform selections, but you'll find that oftentimes, while drawing your selection, you'll need to draw a perfectly straight segment, even for just a few pixels. You can do just that by holding the Option key (PC: Alt key), releasing the mouse button, and continuing to draw your selection. You'll notice that your cursor changes to the Polygonal Lasso tool and that as you move the mouse, a perfectly straight selection will drag out. When you've dragged the straight selection where you want, click-and-hold the mouse button (to add a point), release the Option/Alt key, and you'll be back to the regular Lasso tool again. Drag the mouse to continue drawing your selection.

SKIP THE ZOOM TOOL

The Zoom tool is okay to use when you need to zoom in on a particular area, but if you need to zoom out, it stinks. That's because you have to hold the Option key (PC: Alt key) and click on your image, and every time you do, it only zooms outward one step. Want to zoom in and out of your image like a pro? Instead press Command-+ (PC: Control-+) to quickly zoom in, and Command-– (PC: Control-–) to zoom out (that's the minus key for zooming out). Start using this, and you'll only grab the Zoom tool for zoom ins, and then only half as much as you used to.

CAN'T REMEMBER SELECTION SHORTCUTS? LOOK AT THE CURSOR

If you've made a selection and want to add to that selection, just hold the Shift key and you can add more area to it. Of course, we just told you it was the Shift key, but what if you couldn't remember which key it was? Just press a modifier key (such as Shift, Option/Alt, Command/Control, etc.) then look at your cursor. When you hold the Shift key, a little plus sign appears at the bottom right-hand corner of the cursor to tell you that you can now add to the selection. Hold Option (PC: Alt) and a minus sign appears to tell you that you can now subtract from the selection. Hold Command (PC: Control) and a pair of scissors appears, telling you that if you click-and-drag the selection, it will cut out the image inside of the selection and move it right along with the cursor.

YES, THE DEFAULT GRADIENTS ARE LAME

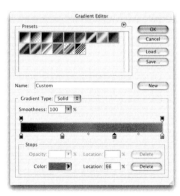

Ever take a look at the default gradients that are loaded in Photoshop's Gradient Picker? Pretty lame. Are you stuck with them? Heaven forbid. To create a custom gradient, get the Gradient tool, then click on the Gradient Sample in the Options Bar to bring up the Gradient Editor. To edit an existing color, double-click on the little house icon under the Gradient Bar (these are called "Color Stops"). To add a Stop, click once under the Gradient Bar and a new Stop will appear. To remove any Stop, click on it and drag straight downward. When you've got a gradient you like, give it a name and then press the New button (I know, that sounds kind of backwards—name it, then press New—but that's how it works).

⊙ ⊙ ⊙ YOUR SELECTIONS AREN'T STUCK—MOVE 'EM!

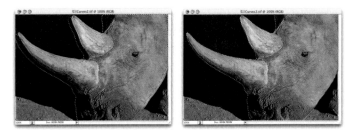

If you've drawn a selection and it didn't quite wind up in the exact spot you wanted, you can move it. The key is making sure you move it with a Selection tool (Lasso, Rectangular Marquee, Magic Wand, etc.), rather than the Move tool. Just move your cursor inside your selected area and you'll notice that it changes to a hollow arrow with a square selection. That's letting you know you're just moving the selection, so now you can drag the selection wherever you want. You can also use the Arrow keys on your keyboard to nudge your selection around if you prefer. If you switch to the Move tool and move the selection, it will move the pixels under your selection, rather than moving the selection itself.

⊙ ⊙ ⊙ WHICH TOOL DO YOU HAVE? PHOTOSHOP CAN TELL YOU

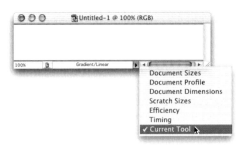

If you're brand-new to Photoshop, it definitely takes a while to learn which tool to use, and even which tool you have selected from the Toolbox. Luckily, Photoshop can tell you which tool you have through the Information box at the bottom left of your document window. To turn this feature on, click-and-hold on the right-facing triangle toward the bottom left-hand side of your image window (shown at left) and choose Current Tool from the pop-up menu. The name of your currently selected tool will appear in the Information box in the left-hand side of your document window.

⬤ ⬤ ⬤ GET RID OF THE ANNOYING CHECKERBOARD PATTERN

Anytime you create a new layer, by default Photoshop puts a checkerboard pattern behind the transparent areas of your layer. The idea is so that you'll know which areas are transparent. We've always felt we had something that would tell us which areas were transparent—our eyes. So we (and many other users) turned this annoying checkerboard off as soon as we learned how. Here's how: In Mac OS X, go under the Photoshop menu, under Preferences, and choose Transparency & Gamut (in Windows and Mac OS 9.x , Preferences can be found under the Edit menu). In the dialog box, change the Grid Size from Medium to None. That's it—click OK and the annoying grid is gone. (Want to play a Photoshop prank? Go to a friend's or coworker's computer and change their Grid Size to Large and the Grid Colors to Dark. If that doesn't send them into rehab, nothing will.)

⬤ ⬤ ⬤ UNDERSTANDING THE GIANT MONDO-BIG BRUSHES PALETTE

If you're freaked out by all the sliders, menus, buttons, and clutter in the new expanded (read incredibly huge behemoth) Brushes palette, I have a tip that will help you to understand how it works so that it will immediately feel more friendly and familiar. Here it is: It works much the same way as the Layer Styles dialog box. That's right. If you look at the Layer Styles dialog, the menu on the left side of it looks, and works, pretty much like the left side menu in the expanded Brushes palette. For example, in the Layer Styles dialog box, to add an effect, you click on the checkbox, but to edit that effect's options, you click on its name. This is the same in the Brushes palette. To add an effect to your current brush, click on the checkbox beside the effect. To edit that effect, click directly on the effects name, and its options appear.

HOW TO TAME THE SELECT SIMILAR COMMAND

A popular trick for making selections of large areas (such as backgrounds) is to select part of the background that contains most of the colors that appear within that background. Then you can go under the Select menu and choose Similar. Photoshop will then select all the similar colors in your image. This can really speed up the task of selecting an entire background, especially if the background is limited to just a few colors. Here's the tip: Do you know what determines how many pixels out the Similar command selects? Believe it or not, it's controlled by the Magic Wand's Tolerance setting. The higher the setting, the more pixels it selects. Eerie, ain't it? Sooooooo… if you use Similar, and it doesn't select enough colors, go to the Magic Wand tool, increase the Tolerance setting, and then try running Similar again. This all makes perfect sense (at least to an engineer at Adobe).

RUN THAT FILTER ONE MORE TIME

Once you've applied a filter to your image, Photoshop thoughtfully puts that filter at the top of the list in your Filter menu, just in case you decide to run that exact same filter again, with the exact same settings. That way, you don't have to go digging through your Filter submenus tracking it down to run it again. However, even more convenient is the keyboard shortcut that lets you run it again without going to the Filter menu at all. It's Command-F (PC: Control-F). What if you don't want the same settings (ahhh, I knew you were going to ask that)? Try pressing Command-Option-F (PC: Control-Alt-F), which brings up the dialog box for the last filter you applied with the last settings that you used.

REDOCKING THE FILE BROWSER

Photoshop 7.0's File Browser lives (by default) in the Options Bar's Palette Well, where you can easily access it in one click. You can also drag the File Browser tab from the Palette Well so that it floats separately like any other palette. But here's the catch—try to "redock" it. Wait! Whoa! Where's the little tab you normally grab

to dock a palette into the Palette Well? There is no tab for the File Browser, so how do you get it "redocked?" Just go to the File Browser's pop-down menu and choose Dock to Palette Well, and it will dutifully jump back up to where it belongs, patiently waiting for its next mission.

WANT THE DEFAULT COLORS? JUST "D-DO" IT

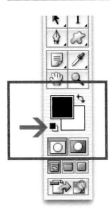

Photoshop's default setting for the Foreground color is black, and the default for the Background color is white. There is a tiny little icon below and to the left of your Foreground/Background swatches in the Toolbox that lets you return to those defaults anytime by clicking on it, but there's actually a faster way than making the trip to the Toolbox—just press the letter "d" on your keyboard.

⬤ ⬤ ⬤ COLOR CORRECTION FOR DUMMIES

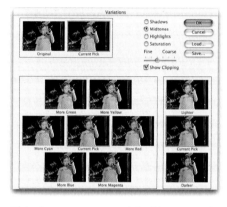

If you don't have any experience in correcting images (i.e., you open an image, it looks pretty bad, and you don't know what to do next), try this: Go under the Image menu, under Adjustments, and choose Auto Levels. It's not a miracle cure, but in many cases it will make your image have better contrast and more balanced color. If you look at your image and you can easily see that it still has too much of one color or another (i.e., the whole image looks too red, too blue, or even too dark or light), go under the Image Menu, under Adjustments, and choose Variations. This shows you your original image and a number of color-modified versions (variations) of your image. Your job is to click on any of the thumbnail images that looks better than your current image. You don't need any color experience at all—you just have to be able to decide which thumbnail looks better than your original (and usually, that's pretty easy).

⬤ ⬤ ⬤ CAN'T FIND THE AIRBRUSH TOOL? DON'T FREAK OUT

If there's one thing that sends a chill down the spine of Photoshop artists using 7.0, it's finding out that their most exalted and beloved tool, the Airbrush, is missing from the Toolbox. You can see them searching frantically behind each flyout menu, until they come to the stark realization that it's just plain gone. Never fear, Adobe wouldn't take one of the coolest tools in Photoshop away. Instead, what they've done is offer the power of the Airbrush (the ability to control the flow of paint with the mouse or a Wacom pen) to all the brush tools, so any brush can become "an Airbrush," including the Clone Stamp tool, the Eraser, etc. Just choose a brush tool of some sort, and then up in the Options Bar you'll find a button with the icon of the Airbrush tool. Click on it, and your current brush becomes an Airbrush.

HIDE THAT HARSH, NASTY EDGE

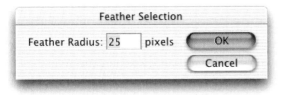

Once you've drawn a few selections and adjusted the selected area, you can often see a visible line along the area you selected. For example, if you selected someone's hand and changed the lightness of their hand, you might see a visible line where their hand meets the rest of their arm, right where your selection was. How do you get around this obvious line? You need to soften the edge of your selection, which makes the transition more smooth, by adding a Feather to your selection. Here's how: Draw your selection, go under the Select menu, and choose Feather. The Feather Selection dialog box will appear, asking you to enter a Feather Radius. The higher the number, the softer your edge will be. Note: You won't see the effect of your feathering until you either move the selected area with the Move tool, adjust the tone, or Copy and Paste it into another document. Because the edge transition is so soft, feathering is often used when combining multiple images for a collage effect.

ESCAPE FROM THE CROP TOOL (OR DIE!)

Sometimes when you're using the Crop tool, you change your mind and decide not to crop. If this happens to you, do you have to crop and then press the undo shortcut? Nah, press the Escape key to cancel your crop and remove the cropping border. You can also click on the "x" icon on the far right of the Options Bar to cancel a crop as well. Okay, there's one more way, just switch tools—a dialog box will appear asking you if you want to complete the crop or not. Just hit Don't Crop.

BRUSHES PALETTE: THAT'S NOT A HEADER, IT'S A BUTTON

If you look in the expanded Brushes palette, there's a list of controls on the left side of the dialog. At the top it reads "Brush Presets," and you might figure that you can click on that and get some options, but the one that catches just about everyone off guard is just below that. It's the header for "Brush Tip Shape." It appears to be a header for a list of brush tip options below it, but in reality, it's a button (I know, it doesn't look like a button, but it is). Click right on the word "Brush Tip Shape" and the Brush Tip Shape options are revealed in the main panel.

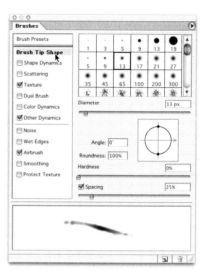

DANGEROUS INTERSECTION?

You've already learned that if you're using a selection tool (Lasso, Rectangular Marquee, etc.) and you need to add an additional area to your currently selected area, you can hold the Shift key, then any selection you draw with one of those tools will be added. But what if you have a selection and instead you want to create a new selection that will intersect with your existing selection to create an entirely new selection (Whew! That's sounds complicated just explaining it). Here's how: Draw your first selection, then up in the Options Bar you'll find four icons for various selection options. The fourth icon is called "Intersect with Selection." Click on it, then draw another selection that overlaps your existing selection and all will become clear (grasshopper).

⬤ ⬤ ⬤ NUDGING YOUR WAY AROUND

As long as you have the Move tool selected, you can move (called nudging) your current layer using the Up/Down/Left/Right Arrow keys on your keyboard. For every press of an Arrow, it nudges your layer 1 pixel in that direction. If you hold the Shift key and use the Arrow keys, it nudges the object 10 pixels at a time.

⬤ ⬤ ⬤ MAKE THAT OPTIONS BAR FLOAT—FLOAT???

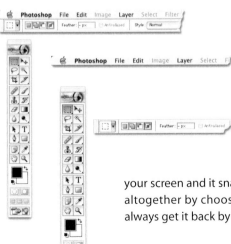

You may not realize it, but the Options Bar, which seems permanently docked to the top of your work area, can actually be redocked to the bottom of your screen, or you can make it into a floating palette. To make it float, just click on the little tab on the far-left side of the bar and drag it away and voilà—it floats. To dock it at the bottom of your screen, drag the tab down to the bottom left-hand side of your screen and it snaps into place. You can even hide the Options Bar altogether by choosing "Options" from the Window menu. You can always get it back by double-clicking on any tool.

PROTECT YOUR ORIGINAL IMAGE

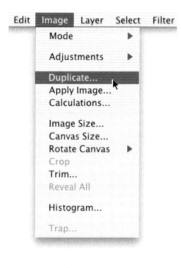

Afraid of doing some irreparable damage to your image (don't feel bad, we all are)? Then make a duplicate of it by going under the Image menu and choosing Duplicate. An exact duplicate (including any layers, paths, etc.) will be created with the word "copy" at the end of its name. Do with it what you will.

KILL THE PALETTES!

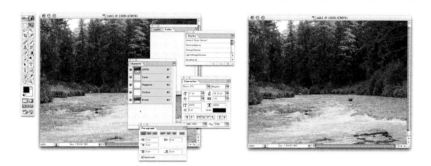

Is your Photoshop work area looking too cluttered? Is there a palette covering every inch of free space and half of the image you're working on? Anytime you get to this stage (and yes, you'll get to this stage), you can temporarily hide all your palettes by pressing the Tab key. Want 'em back? Just press Tab again.

SUPERSIZE IT

This is a super speed trick for getting your image view up (or down) to size. To instantly view your image at 100% size, double-click on the Zoom tool in the Toolbox. To have your image fit as large as possible on your screen (called "Fit On Screen"), double-click the Hand tool.

LOCK THOSE PIXELS AND FILL

This is a great timesaving shortcut when you have an object on a layer, and you want to fill just the object with the Foreground color (rather than filling the entire layer with color). Press Shift-Option-Delete (PC: Shift-Alt-Backspace). What this does is turn on Lock Transparent Pixels for the layer in the Layers palette, fills the object on your layer, and then turns Lock Transparent Pixels back off. What if you want to fill your object with a gradient? It's a little more laborious. Turn on Lock Transparent Pixels by using the Forward Slash key (/) shortcut. Drag your Gradient tool through your object, and then press Forward Slash (/) again to turn off Lock Transparent Pixels.

STEAL COLOR FROM ANYWHERE

In all previous versions of Photoshop, you could click the Eyedropper tool on any color within your image, and it would steal that color and make it your new Foreground color. The only drawback was, you could only steal colors from within an open document window—that is until now. In Photoshop 7.0, Adobe cut the Eyedropper tool loose from the chains that bound it, and now, as long as you click within an open image first, you can drag right out of your image window and sample a color from, well, anywhere. That includes sam-

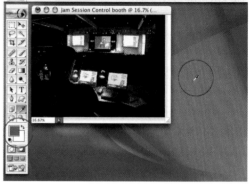

pling colors from other applications, Photoshop's own Toolbox and menu bars, and even your computer's desktop pattern. Just remember to click in your image first, and then drag that Eyedropper to a new world of color delights that dare not speak its name.

ASK PHOTOSHOP TO REMEMBER MORE

Photoshop remembers the last 30 documents that you had open, but by default it only displays the last four under the File menu, under Open Recent. However, you're not limited to just four. Would you rather Photoshop displayed the last eight instead? Then in Mac OS X, go under the Photoshop menu, under Preferences, and choose File Handling (in Windows and Mac OS 9.x, Preferences can be found under the Edit menu). When the dialog box appears, under "Recent File List Contains," enter the desired number of files (up to 30) that you want to have quick access to under the Open Recent menu.

THE MONDO-COOL BATCH RANKING SECRET SHORTCUT

If you're using Photoshop 7.0's File Browser, you're probably already using the handy ranking system, where you can sort your images by ranking the best images, then the second best, third best, etc. If you have a lot of images, this can really take some time, but if you use this cool hidden little tip (shown to me by Adobe's own graphics evangelist and undisputed Queen of Photoshop, Julieanne Kost), you can make quick work

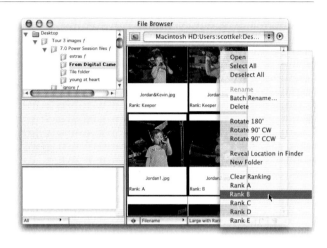

of it (whatever that means). Here's how: Open the File Browser, and then Shift-click on all the images you want to share a similar rank (like all the best images in a particular folder of images). Then, Control-click (PC: Right-click) in one of those Shift-clicked images and a pop-up menu will appear, and when you choose a ranking for this one image, all the Shift-clicked images will automatically share the same ranking, saving you a boatload of time (which frankly is a time measurement that is vastly underused).

SHRINK THOSE PALETTES DOWN TO SIZE

Are your palettes in the way, but you don't want to hide them all using the Tab key (like we mentioned earlier)? You can double-click the palette's name tab, and the palette will minimize down to just the tab itself, giving you back lots of screen real estate. Need the palette back, just double-click on its tab again.

SHOW ME THE EXTRAS

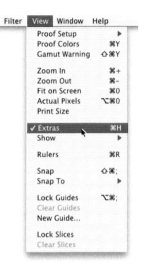

Photoshop has all sorts of little visual helpers to let you work more efficiently, such as grids, guides, selection edges, etc. Adobe calls these "extras" because they charge you extra for them (kidding). You can toggle these visual helpers off and on by choosing Extras from the View menu, or by using the keyboard shortcut Command-H (PC: Control-H). The cool thing is that you have control over which "extras" are hidden and which remain visible when you choose Extras by going under the View Menu, under Show, and choosing Show Extras Options from the bottom of the list. A dialog box will appear with checkboxes for the extras you want affected by toggling on/off Extras.

CREATING THE ÜBER PALETTE

You've been able to nest one or more palettes into another palette since back in Photoshop 3.0. No big deal, but now you can not only nest but you can also dock palettes one atop the other, creating a giant über palette. Here's how: Drag the name tab of one palette to the bottom edge of a second palette and slowly drag upward. A thin black double-line will appear at the bottom of the top palette letting you know its "time to dock." Release the mouse and your palettes will be docked, one on top of the other. Now, when you move the top palette, all docked palettes will move with it as a group. We use this feature to stack our Character and Paragraph palettes so we can access all our type settings in one place.

KILLING LAYERS WITH NO MERCY

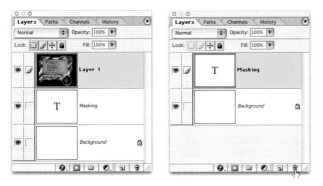

Want to delete a layer with as much speed and prejudice as possible? Try this: Hold the Option key (PC: Alt key) and click on the Trash icon at the bottom of the Layers palette. Bang—it's gone. No warning dialog, no muss, no fuss. If you hold Shift-Option-Esc-F13-Control-Delete-Page Up, it will even drive the layer out to the docks and dump it in the East River.

 TIRED OF PRESSING THE SHIFT KEY TO ROTATE THROUGH TOOLS?

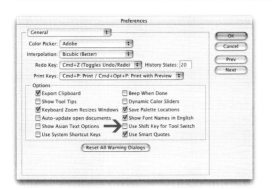

Back in the old days, there just weren't that many tools in Photoshop, and if you wanted to rotate through the various tools (say the Pen tool for instance), you'd just press the letter "p" over and over again until the Pen tool you wanted made its way to the Toolbox. Ah, those were simpler times. But as Photoshop 5.0, 5.5, 6.0, and now 7.0 came about, so did more tools, and now by default you also have to press Shift to rotate through the tools. Or do you? Hmmmm.

Actually, you can request (politely) that Photoshop let you revert to the ways of old, allowing you to press just one key to rotate through the tools. You do this in Mac OS X by going under the Photoshop menu, under Preferences, and choosing General (in Windows and Mac OS 9.x, Preferences can be found under the Edit menu). In that dialog, uncheck the box for "Use Shift Key for Tool Switch." It's like stepping back in time.

CHAPTER 2 • Essential Tips You've Got to Know 45

FIX THOSE TOOL SETTINGS FAST

There's no doubt you'll be "messing" with many, if not all, of the options for the tools you use every day in Photoshop. One day you'll go to use a tool, and you'll have messed with it to the extent that something's just not right. To quickly get back to any tool's default settings, choose the tool from the Toolbox, then Control-click (PC: Right-click) on the tool's icon that appears up in the Options Bar at the far left. A pop-up menu will appear, where you can choose Reset Tool to set it back to its factory-fresh defaults. By the way, while you're there, you can also choose Reset All Tools and they will all revert to their defaults as well.

BRING ORDER BACK TO YOUR WORLD

In Photoshop, you're constantly moving your palettes around, and before long, you've got one messy set of palettes littering your screen. If your palettes get messy, you're only one simple menu command from having them back at their factory-fresh default locations. Just go under the Window menu, under Workspace, and choose Reset Palette Locations, and all will be right with your world once again (that is, until you mess 'em up again).

THE UNDOCUMENTED FILL SHORTCUT

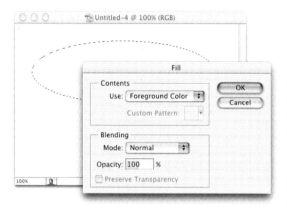

There are all sorts of keyboard shortcuts for filling selections, entire layers, and stuff like that, but if you look under the Edit menu, next to the Fill command, there doesn't appear to be a shortcut for bringing up the Fill dialog box itself. Luckily, there's an undocumented keyboard shortcut that will do the trick—it's Shift-Delete (PC: Shift-Backspace). This is a good one to pull on your Photoshop buddies and coworkers as a Photoshop trivia question, because few people know it exists.

DESELECTED AND FORGOT TO SAVE? DON'T SWEAT IT

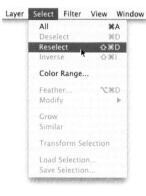

If, after you created a selection in an image, deselected it, and moved on to other things, you suddenly wish you had that selection back, you're not out of luck. As long as you haven't made another selection (since the one you want to get back), Photoshop remembers your last selection and lets you get it back by going under the Select menu and choosing Reselect. When you choose it, the last selection you created reappears within your image. If you create a selection that, while it's still active, you know you want to keep for later use, then go under the Select menu and choose Save Selection. When the Save Selection dialog box appears, click OK, and Photoshop saves it. You can reload it anytime by going under the Select menu and choosing Load Selection. Your selection will be named "Alpha 1" by default, and you can choose to load it (or other subsequent saved selections) from the pop-up menu in the Load Selection dialog box.

⚫ ⚫ ⚫ SUPER FAST INCHES TO PIXELS

Want to change the unit of measurement for your image? Don't go digging through Photoshop's menus for the Preferences dialog, just Control-click (PC: Right-click) on Photoshop's rulers and a pop-up menu will appear with a list of measurement units. Choose the one you want, and your rulers will instantly reflect the change. If you feel you must access the Units & Rulers preferences dialog, just double-click anywhere on one of Photoshop's rulers and the dialog will appear.

⚫ ⚫ ⚫ LIGHTNING-FAST FEATHER

If you're using the Lasso tool and want to add a feather to soften the edges of the selection, there's no faster way than this: Hit the Return key (PC: Enter key) and the Feather field in the Options Bar will highlight. Then all you have to do is enter the value for how much feathering you want (just remember to set the feathering back to zero when you're done, using the same shortcut).

⬤ ⬤ ⬤ BOSS AROUND YOUR COLOR SWATCHES

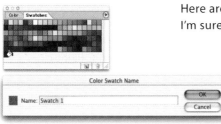

Here are a few tips for using the Swatches palette. I'm sure you know that if you click on a color in the Swatches palette, that color becomes your new Foreground color. Here's one you may not have realized—if you Command-click (PC: Control-click) on a swatch, that color now becomes your Background color. Also, you can delete any swatch by holding the Option key (PC: Alt key) and clicking on the swatch you want to remove. You can also add a color to your swatches by setting your Foreground color to the color you want to save, then hold the Shift key and click on any open space in the Swatches palette.

⬤ ⬤ ⬤ ZOOMED IN? DON'T USE THE SCROLL BARS

If you've zoomed in on an image, using the scroll bars can be incredibly frustrating, because you move just a tiny bit. Here's how to get around that—don't use the scroll bars (okay, there's more to it than that). Instead, when you're zoomed in, use the Hand tool, but to save time, access it by simply pressing the Spacebar. It temporarily switches you to the Hand, letting you easily navigate through your zoomed image.

LET PHOTOSHOP DO THE MATH WHEN COPYING/PASTING

If you've selected something within your Photoshop document and you want to copy and paste that item into its own separate document, don't worry about typing in the Width and Height into Photoshop's New document dialog box. Photoshop automatically figures that you're going to paste that image into a new document, so when you open the New dialog box, the exact size of your copied selection has already been entered for you, so just click OK, and then paste your image inside—it'll be a perfect fit.

INSTANT SELECTION FROM ANY PATH

When you're using the Pen tool to create a path, you can go to the Paths palette and click on the third icon from the left (at the bottom of the palette) to turn your path into a selection, or you can use the keyboard shortcut Command-Return (PC: Control-Enter). We prefer the keyboard shortcut, because it will do the exact same job faster and saves us from opening the Paths palette, taking up valuable screen real estate.

THE COOLEST FILE FORMAT

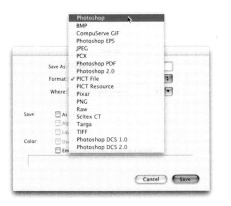

Not sure which file format you should save in?
Try Photoshop's native format (choose Photoshop
from the Format pop-up menu in the Save As
dialog). This format is ideal if you're going to
be working on this file again in Photoshop, or if
Photoshop is the only application this image will
be used in (in other words, you're going to print
directly out of Photoshop and you're not placing
the file into QuarkXPress, Adobe InDesign, or
PageMaker for output).

Photoshop format compresses the file without
any loss of quality, and this format maintains all
the layers in your image, as well as any paths or channels you've created. However, only other
Adobe products (such as Adobe After Effects) support opening of Photoshop native files.
As long as you're *not* going to import this file into other non-Adobe apps, it's usually pretty safe
to use the Photoshop format to save your file.

BRING YOUR DOCUMENTS DOWN TO SIZE

When you're working with a layered image,
objects on any given layer can extend beyond
the canvas of your document. That's a great
thing, and allows lots of design flexibility,
but the downside is that even though you
can't see all of the objects on a layer, the
hidden part still contributes to the overall
size of your document. Here's how to trim that
size down in a hurry. As long as you're sure
you won't need to pull those non-visible parts
of those layers back into your image, press
Command-A (PC: Control-A) to select your
entire image, then go under the Image menu
and choose Crop, and that will trim away all the hidden areas and get your file back down to a
reasonable size. After all, why keep all that extra girth if you're not going to use it?

● ● ● SAVE CLICKS WHEN YOU CLOSE

This is such a quick little tip that you might not think that it matters, but it saves a few seconds every time you close a document. If you close a number of documents a day (and my guess is, you do), it really starts to add up fast. When you close a document, Photoshop presents you with a dialog box asking, "Save changes to the Adobe Photoshop document before closing?" You have three choices: (1) Don't Save, (2) Cancel, and (3) Save. Here's the shortcut: Press the letter "d" for Don't Save, press "s" for Save, and "c" for Cancel.

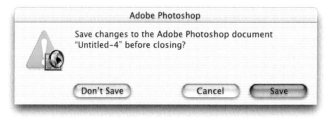

● ● ● BEEN BINGEING ON RAM? MAYBE IT'S TIME TO PURGE!

What do you do if the dreaded "Not enough RAM to complete this function" dialog box appears? Outside of buying more RAM and installing it on the spot, you might want to purge some of the "junk" hanging around in RAM so you can free up some space to complete the project you're working on. You do this by going under the Edit menu, under Purge, and choosing to empty either your Undo, Photoshop's Clipboard, your History States, or everything at once (All). They're in the order you should proceed, so first try purging your Undo and see if that frees up enough memory. If that doesn't do it, try the Clipboard, then Histories. If that doesn't do it, try this super-slick insider tip: Make a tiny (1x1") selection within your document, and then go under the Edit menu and choose Copy three times in a row. Believe it or not, it often works, and has gotten us out of more than one sticky situation.

IF IT SOUNDS LIKE THE TOOL, IT PROBABLY IS

There are a few tool shortcuts that are really worth memorizing—one, because they'll save you time and trips to the Toolbox, and two, because they're so easy. Here are the five you should learn right off the bat:

The Move tool (press the letter "v")
The Pen tool (press the letter "p")
The Lasso tool (press the letter "l")
The Rectangular Marquee tool (press the letter "m")
The Type tool (press the letter "t")

Two others you should commit to memory (that aren't tool tips) are "d" for resetting your Foreground color to black, and "d" then "x" for setting your Foreground color to white.

TRANSFORMING AND COPYING AT THE SAME TIME

Generally, when you apply a transformation to an object (scaling, rotating, distorting, perspective), you apply that transformation to the object itself. However, here's a cool tip if you want to apply a transformation (using Free Transform) on a duplicate of your object, rather than on the original: Press Option-Command-T (PC: Alt-Control-T), then use the Free Transform tool as you usually would. You'll notice that as you begin to transform, the original object remains untouched, and a copy is transformed instead.

THE SMALLER TOOLBOX TRICK

Is that Toolbox taking up too much space, but you don't want to close it, because a few seconds later, sure enough, you'll need a tool? Then just double-click on the very top of your Toolbox and it will tuck up out of the way, leaving just that little tab showing. Need it back fast, just double-click the little tab again and it comes right back.

SNAP YOUR PALETTES TO ORDER

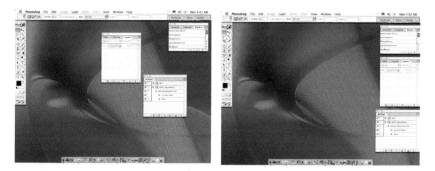

If you like order in your world, then you'll love this tip for making your palettes snap to the edge of your screen. Just hold the Shift key and click on the topmost bar of your palette and it will snap to the closest edge (left, right, top, or bottom), bringing order and harmony to your workspace once again. Ahhhhh.

ONE-BUTTON REFRESH FOR THE FILE BROWSER

When you're ranking images in 7.0's File Browser, you've probably noticed that the sorting (by rank) doesn't happen automatically as you rank each image—you have to either change your "Sort By" pop-up menu at the bottom of the File Browser to a different choice (like Filename) and then switch back to Rank, or you have to choose Refresh Desktop View from the File Browser's pop-down menu. Either way, unless you're charging by the hour, it just takes too long. Instead, just press F5 for an instant refresh anytime.

DON'T LET THE BROWSER PREVIEW FOOL YOU

When you rotate an image in the File Browser, Photoshop doesn't actually rotate the file until you open the image, so all you're really rotating is the preview. If you want the image permanently rotated, you have to open the image, let Photoshop rotate it, and then resave it. Only then will the image become permanently rotated. Otherwise, you're just telling Photoshop, "Hey, when you open this image, rotate it for me, okay?" It just saves you a step.

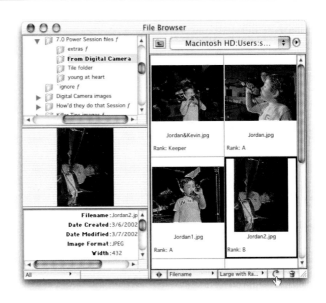

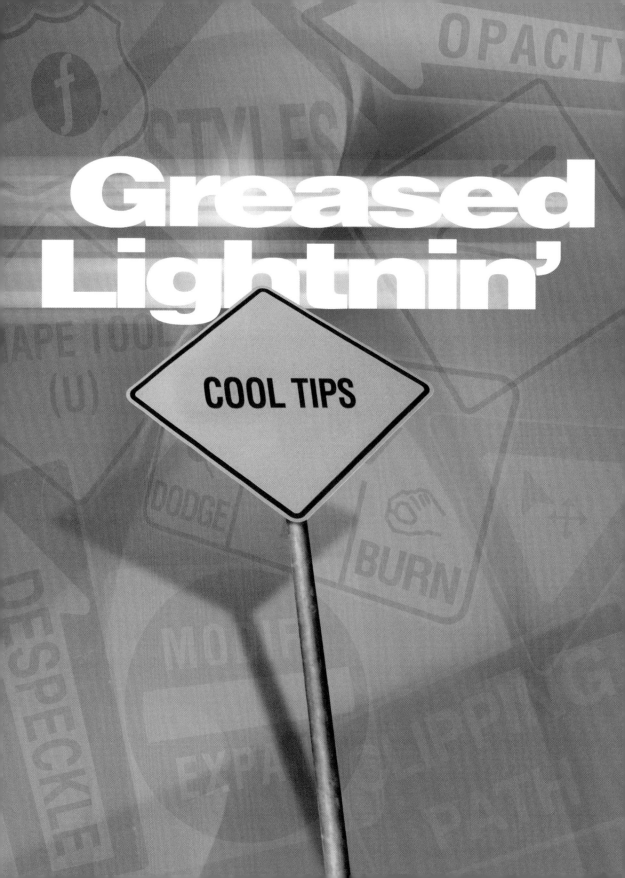

Greased Lightnin'

COOL TIPS

Why is this chapter named "Way Cool Tips?" It's because "Boring Regular Tips" was already taken (psyche!). Actually, it's because this is where

Greased Lightnin'

way cool tips

a lot of the really cool tips wound up that didn't fit into any of the other categories. I don't really have anything else to say about this chapter, so instead, let's fill this space by singing a verse of "Greased Lightnin'" from the motion picture Grease.

"We'll get some overhead lifters, and four-barrel quads, oh yeah (keep talkin', whoa, keep talkin'). Fuel-injection cutoff and chrome-plated rods, oh yeah (I'll get the money, I'll see you get the money), with the four-speed on the floor, they'll be waitin' at the door, you know that ain't no…" Hey, wait a minute—that next word is a cuss word. Okay, no problem, we'll skip over that word and continue, "…we'll be getting lots of…." Gees, another nasty word. I've been singing that song for years and never really noticed how nasty it was. Just to be safe, let's just jump to the end of the chorus, "…you know that I ain't braggin', she's a real…." Oh, that's just wrong! I'm stopping right here.

MORE GRADIENT COLOR STOPS THAN YOU CAN SHAKE A STICK AT

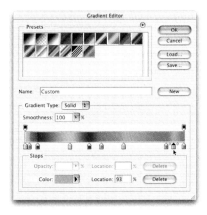

Here's the scenario: You're making a custom gradient and you need to duplicate one or more of the Color Stops. No problem. Once you've created one gradient Color Stop, you can make copies by Option-dragging it (PC: Alt-dragging). Also, as long as you keep the Option key (PC: Alt key) down while you drag, you can jump right over other existing Stops. It's a Color Stop love fest, can you feel it?

TO DEFRINGE, OR NOT TO DEFRINGE, THAT IS THE QUESTION

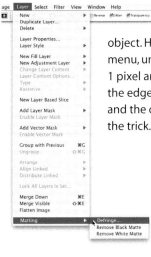

Anytime you're creating a collage, you'll eventually add an image that has little white pixels around the edges of your object. Here's a tip for getting rid of that "fringe." Go under the Layer menu, under Matting, and choose Defringe. Try the default setting of 1 pixel and click OK. What this does (here's the techno speak) is replace the edge pixels with a combination of the pixel colors in your object and the colors in the background (whew, that hurt). That usually does the trick. If it doesn't, undo it, then try a 2- or 3-pixel Defringe.

CRACKING THE EASTER EGG MYSTERY

Easter Eggs are usually funny little messages hidden within an application (engineer humor just cracks us up). Photoshop has a few of its own, but one of the lesser-known Easter Eggs is "Merlin Lives." To see this Easter Egg, go to the Paths palette, hold the Option key (PC: Alt key), and in the palette's pop-down menu, choose Palette Options. When you do, a tiny floating palette will appear with a picture of Merlin and just one button named "Begone," which closes the dialog. I've got to party with those engineer guys.

SUPERCHARGE YOUR FILTER EFFECTS

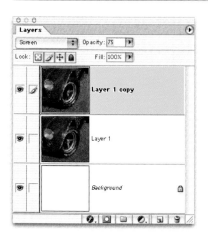

Next time before you apply a cool filter to an image, instead of just selecting an area and applying the filter, press Command-J (PC: Control-J) to put your selected area up on its own layer. What's the advantage of this? Well first, it gives you more control over the effect. For example, by having the area on its own layer, after you apply the filter, you can then change the Blend Modes of the layer to get even more out of the filters (multiplying it, screening it, overlaying it, etc.). And secondly, you have control of your filter "after the fact." If, after you applied the filter, you felt it was too intense, you could always lower the Opacity of the layer to calm it down a bit.

UNDO ON A SLIDER!

If you apply a technique (such as a filter or a paint stroke) and the effect is too intense, you can always undo the effect by pressing Command-Z (PC: Control-Z). But if you just want to decrease the intensity, instead of completely undoing it, go under Edit, and choose Fade. Want a less intense effect? Just move the slider to the left. The farther you drag, the less intense the effect. Drag all the way to the left, and the effect is undone.

NEW RENAMING POWER

One of our favorite features in Photoshop 7.0 (and this is going to sound silly) is the simple way you can now rename layers. I know, I know, but we can't help it—we love the simplicity of it. And although Adobe made a big deal about this new layer-renaming scheme (and well they should), what they haven't made a big deal about is the fact that they didn't stop with just the Layers palette. You can also rename Styles, Color Swatches in the Swatches palette, brushes in the Brushes palette, Action names, and even snapshots in the History palette (basically any palette than can show palette items in "text only" mode, rather than just swatches or buttons) the same way—just double-click on the name, the field highlights, and type in the new name.

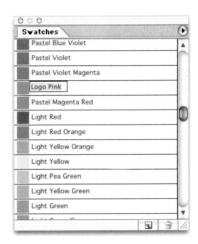

 **TWO FILES ARE BETTER THAN ONE**

There are times when we should be working (or experimenting) on a copy of an image—it's a shame to trash a good image and then try to re-create it. You could always do a Save As and choose As a Copy, but here's a better way: Go to the bottom of the History palette and click on the Create New Snapshot icon (the one that looks like a camera). Click on the new snapshot near the top of the History palette to make it the active History state. Finally, go to the bottom of the History palette and click on the Create New Document from Current State icon. There you go, a copy of the image, just dying for you to trash it.

 **RESIZING PATHS THE EASY WAY**

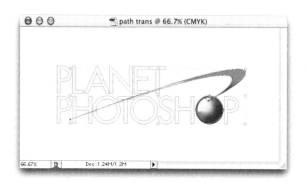

When you're using the Pen tool, you can visually resize your path by using the Path Selection tool. To do this, go up in the Options Bar and turn on the checkbox for Show Bounding Box. This puts a Free Transform-like bounding box around your path, and you can use this bounding box to resize your path by dragging the handles (remember to hold the Shift key to resize it proportionately).

LET THOSE WINDOWS BREATHE!

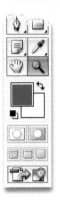

Since Photoshop 3.0, Photoshop has done something called "protecting the palettes" (I don't know if that's its official name, but we've always heard it called that). What that means is that as you increase the size of your image, Photoshop automatically stops increasing the size of the image window when it reaches the left edge of your open palettes. When it reaches this safety zone, the window stops growing, and only the image within the window continues to zoom. The only way to get around this (in previous versions of Photoshop) was to close your palettes. Then you could zoom the window as large as you'd like. However, Adobe addressed this problem back in Photoshop 6, and now if you want to keep the window growing, click on the Zoom tool, and up in the Options Bar, choose Ignore Palettes.

THE MULTIPLE UNDO SHORTCUT

Need to back up a few steps to readjust a setting? Piece of cake. Here's a shortcut to do just that. You can step back through your History palette by pressing Command-Option-Z (PC: Control-Alt-Z). This doesn't delete the items, but takes you back a step in the History palette.

WANT ARROWHEADS? PHOTOSHOP CAN ADD THEM FOR YOU!

This one is pretty slick because it's been a feature in Photoshop for a while, but eight out of ten Photoshop users will tell you Photoshop can't create arrowheads on the ends of lines (if it makes you feel any better, nine out of ten dentists didn't think Photoshop could do it either). Here's how: First, go under the Shape tools (in the Toolbox) and choose the Line tool. Then, up in the Options Bar, you'll see icons for the six shape tools. Directly to the right of these six icons is a down-facing triangle. Click on that triangle and out pops a dialog where you can click a checkbox to add arrowheads to either the beginning or end of your line, and you can choose the Width, Length, and even the Concavity (there's that dentist thing again).

SMACK IT, FLIP IT, FREE TRANSFORM IT

The Free Transform tool allows you to do all kinds of crazy stuff like Rotate, Skew, Flip Horizontal, and other cool stuff like that. The problem is, how can you remember all that stuff? Simple: Bring up Free Transform by pressing Command-T (PC: Control-T), then Control-click (PC: Right-click) inside the bounding box, and a pop-up menu will appear with a list of all the transformations you can choose from. You also get access to transformations, such as Flip Horizontal/Vertical, Rotate 180°, and Rotate 90° Clockwise/Counterclockwise, that don't have keyboard shortcuts at all.

DRAGGING AND DROPPING WHERE YOU WANT

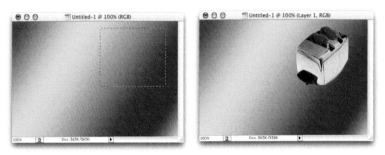

If you drag an image from one document to another, the dragged image appears right at the spot where you let go of the mouse button. You may know that if you hold the Shift key when you drag-and-drop the image, the dragged image will automatically be centered within the receiving image. But you can go one better—make a selection in the receiving document, then hold the Shift key before you drag. Your image will be centered within the selection, instead of within the entire document. Scary, isn't it? You can also copy and paste the selection and Photoshop will center the pasted image in the selection.

CUSTOM BRUSHES DON'T HAVE TO BE SQUARE ANYMORE

In all previous versions of Photoshop, if you wanted to create your own custom brush, there was only one method—draw a square selection around the object that you wanted to become your custom brush, and then choose Define Brush under the Edit menu. In 7.0, Adobe takes the chains off, and now not only can you use irregular selections to define a brush shape (like our crushed can here) you can also even use feathered selections. When the Brush Name dialog box appears, name your brush and click OK. Your new brush will be added to the bottom of your Brushes palette.

FEATHER A SELECTION WITHOUT THE GUESSING GAME

Most of us try to guess how many pixels will give us the nice, soft selection we're looking for when we use the Feather Selection dialog box. Sometimes we guess right, and other times we press Command-Z (PC: Control-Z) to undo the damage before trying again. Try this instead: Make your selection first, and then press "q" to turn on the Quick Mask mode. Now make the edge fade out by going under Filter, under Blur, and choosing Gaussian Blur. You can see how much of a blur you'll need to soften the edges as you adjust the Radius amount. When you're done, press "q" to get back to Standard mode with the selection already made with the exact amount of feathering that you want.

CREATING A FLATTENED VERSION OF YOUR LAYERED IMAGE

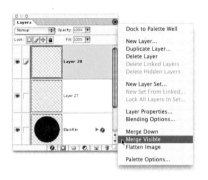

Alright, you're working on a Photoshop file that has a "bizillion" layers, and you want to create a new layer that's an exact copy of what your flattened image would look like. First, create a new blank layer by clicking on the New Layer icon at the bottom of the Layers palette, then hold Option (PC: Alt) and from the Layers palette's pop-down menu, choose Merge Visible. The new layer you created will now have a flattened version of your image appear on that layer.

IF IT'S NOT SQUARE, YOU CAN STILL CROP IT

Want to crop an image, but the area you want to keep is not a perfect square? Don't sweat it—just make a selection around the area you want to keep, using any selection tool you like (even the Lasso tool), and then choose Crop from the Image menu. It will crop the image as tightly as possible.

TOP-SECRET PHOTOSHOP SPLASH SCREEN

If you want to see the secret Photoshop beta start-up screen (the pre-release version of Photoshop 7.0), just hold the Command key (PC: Control key) and choose "About Photoshop." It will show you the splash screen, displaying 7.0's secret pre-release code name. I'm telling you, those engineers know how to party.

FALL IN LOVE WITH A TEMPORARY BRUSH, OR NOT

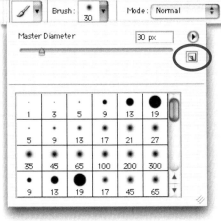

You can create a temporary brush anytime in Photoshop 7.0 by playing with the options in the Brushes palette. After you make your choices, start painting. When you switch to another brush, the temporary brush you just created is gone. If you fall in love with your temporary brush (which is considered illegal in 48 states) and want to save it, before you change brush sizes, click on the Brush Sample up in the Options Bar, and when the Brush Picker appears, click on the New Preset Brush icon in the upper right-hand corner, you sick pup.

 UNDO A SAVE? THAT'S IMPOSSIBLE, ISN'T IT?

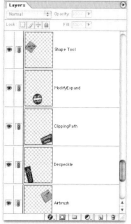

This is a great trick we learned from our buddy Mike Ninness, and the first time we saw it, we said, "Hey, wait a minute, that can't be." Oh, but it be. It's how to undo a Save. This is especially helpful after you've flattened an image, saved the file, then realized that you needed to change something on a layer. This only happens to us about every other day, and here's the keyboard shortcut to fix it: Option-Command-Z (PC: Alt-Control-Z). Press it a few times after you've flattened and saved, and look in your Layers palette to see all the layers come a-rumbling right back. Pretty slick stuff.

MAKE A PHOTOSHOP CLIENT PRESENTATION

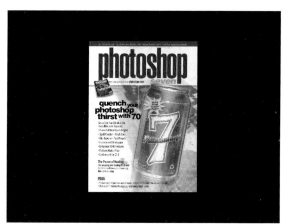

To hide all your palettes and all your menus, and to display your current image centered on your monitor with a cool black frame around your image, just press the letter "f" twice, then press the Tab key (f, f, Tab). To return to your regular Photoshop work area, press "f," then Tab. You'll be the envy of all your friends, and eventually they'll write folk songs about you. It's almost embarrassing.

CHANGE BRUSH SOFTNESS ON-THE-FLY

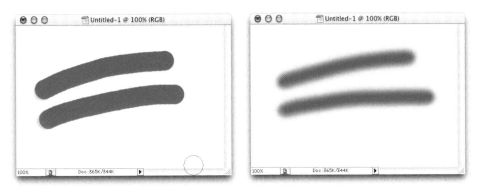

You can increase or decrease the softness of a round brush in Photoshop without changing the size of the brush by pressing Shift-Left Bracket or Shift–Right Bracket. That's almost too easy.

LIGHTS, CAMERA, ACTION: SLIDE SHOWS USING PHOTOSHOP

You can create a mock slide show presentation by opening multiple images in Photoshop and then typing Control-Tab to rotate through the images. Plus, you can hold the Shift key and click on the Full Screen Mode icon near the bottom of your Toolbox to allow your images to fill the full screen (holding Shift will switch all of you open images to the Full Screen Mode at once). Finally, press Tab to hide your palettes and you're all set to give a slick presentation.

LIGHTNING-QUICK COLOR CORRECTION

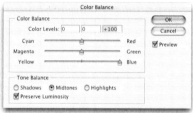

Let's say you have an image, but the sky doesn't look as vibrant as you'd like, and you want to increase the amount of blue without affecting the rest of the image. Try this on for size: Open an image that contains a daylight sky. Click on the New Adjustment Layer icon at the bottom of the Layers palette. In the pop-up menu, choose Color Balance. In the Color Balance dialog box, drag the Blue all the way to the right (it looks bad now, but trust me), and click OK. Now, switch to the Paintbrush tool. Press the letter "d" to set your Foreground color to black, and with a large, soft brush, start painting over the areas you *don't* want blue. As you paint, the blue Color Balance you added is painted away. The sky is much bluer, but you can paint away the added blue from the other areas. To really see the before/after difference, click the Eye icon next to the Adjustment layer.

BUILDING A BETTER BACKGROUND ERASER TOOL

Here's a tip for making Photoshop's Background Eraser tool much more effective. Choose the Background Eraser tool, and in the Options Bar, lower the Tolerance setting to 20. In the Brushes palette, pick a large, hard-edged brush. Then, switch to the Pen tool to draw a path just outside the edge of the object you want to isolate (you don't have to be precise; in fact, stay just outside the edges of the object and draw straight lines all the way around the image). Go to the Paths palette, and in the palette's pop-down menu, choose Stroke Path. When the dialog box appears, under Tool, choose Background Eraser and click OK. The Background Eraser will instantly trace around your image, following the path you created. Now that the edges have been erased, you can use the regular Eraser tool to erase the rest of the background area.

GETTING ANGRIER CLOUDS

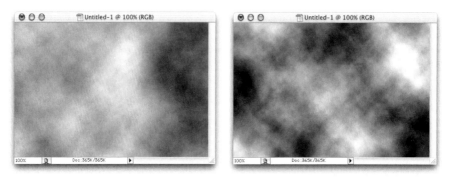

You've probably already played around with the Clouds filter (found under the Render menu), but here's a cool little tip for creating more intense (read angrier) clouds. Hold the Option key (PC: Alt key) before choosing Clouds, and it creates darker, more intense clouds.

CUSTOM BRUSHES: START WITH A CLEAN SLATE

If you're going to build your own custom brush in Photoshop 7.0, sometimes it's easier to start with an existing brush and edit it. The problem is that you may have all sorts of settings already in place (Texture, Scattering, Shape Dynamics, etc. along with

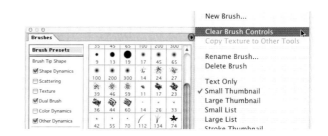

all their individual options). To set everything back to their defaults could take a while. At least it would if you didn't know this cool little trick: Click on the brush you want to use as your starting point for your custom brush, and in the Brushes palette, click on the options you want to edit (like Texture, Scattering, etc.). Then, from the palette's pop-down menu, choose Clear Brush Controls, and all the selected options will be instantly reset to their default settings.

TIMING IS EVERYTHING!

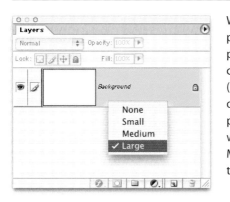

Want to know how long a particular Photoshop command takes? Click on the right-facing triangle toward the bottom left-hand corner of your image window. From the pop-up menu that appears, choose Timing. This starts the equivalent of a stopwatch that times your Photoshop commands in seconds. This is great for speed tests, pitting one machine against another. Which one runs the fastest Unsharp Mask? Time it and find out.

INSTANT THUMBNAIL SIZE CONTROL

Want to change the size of your thumbnail preview in your Layers, Channels, or Paths palettes? Just hold the Control key (PC: Right-click) and click in an open area of the palette (such as the space under your Background layer, or beneath the bottom channel in the Channels palette), and a pop-up menu of thumbnail sizes will appear. You can choose from None, Small, Medium, or Large, instantly changing your thumbnail view.

PREFERENCES SPEED TIP

Do you find yourself using Photoshop's preferences quite often? If you do, you probably know there's a keyboard shortcut to bring the General Preferences up (Command-K/PC: Control-K), but there's actually a cooler tip—how to bring up the last preference dialog you were in. Since Photoshop has eight different preference dialogs, it can save you some significant time digging through the submenus. To bring up the last preference dialog you used, press Option-Command-K (PC: Alt-Control-K).

PHOTO-RETOUCHING SAFETY TIP

Here's a tip that many photo retouchers use—do all your retouching on a layer above your image. That way, you don't damage the underlying image, and you have control over Opacity and Blend Modes you normally wouldn't have. It's also easy to erase areas you wish you hadn't retouched. The key to making this work is to click on the Clone Stamp tool and in the Options Bar, turn on the Use All Layers option. That way you can sample from the underlying image and then paint on the layer above it (believe it or not, by default Photoshop doesn't let you do that—it only lets you clone from the active layer to that same layer).

THE UNDOCUMENTED AIRBRUSH TOGGLE TRICK

This cool, undocumented shortcut comes from our good friend, Web wizard, and all-powerful overlord of every Photoshop keyboard shortcut known to man, Michael Ninness (author of the book *Photoshop 6 Power Shortcuts*, from Que Publishing, ISBN 078972426X). Here's the tip: As you probably know by now, the Airbrush tool is gone from the Toolbox in 7.0, but now you can add Airbrush control to the brush tools by clicking on the Airbrush icon found in the Options Bar of each brush tool (with the exception of the Blur and Sharpen tools—don't ask me why). However, that takes a lot of trips up to the Options Bar. Ah, if only there were a keyboard shortcut that would let you toggle this Airbrush feature on and off at will. Well, there is, and thanks to Michael, we can share it here—it's Shift-Option-P (PC: Shift-Alt-P). Makes you want to buy Michael's book doesn't it? Now, for news of the weird: Although the Dodge, Burn, and Sponge tools enable you to use the Airbrush function, this cool undocumented keyboard shortcut won't work for those three tools. Another unsolved mystery.

NEW DOCUMENTS WITH YOUR CUSTOM SPECS IN 7.0

Photoshop 7.0 introduced a pop-up list of commonly used new document sizes in the New dialog box, and it's a big timesaver, but did you know that you can add your own custom document sizes to the list? It's true, and best of all, the instructions on how to create your own custom new sizes are already on your hard drive. Just look in your Photoshop folder, inside the Presets folder, and you'll find a file named "New Doc Sizes.txt." Open this file (in your favorite text editor or word processor) and follow the step-by-step instructions for adding your own custom sizes to the pop-up list.

Burn Rubber

Do you remember the song "Burn Rubber" by the Gap Band from back in the early '80s? Remember it goes: "Burn rubber on me, Charlene...

Burn Rubber

smokin' type tips

whoa, no...." Not ringing any bells? It doesn't matter. This chapter has nothing to do with burning rubber—I was just curious to see if you're as old as I am (which is young. Very young. I heard that song accidentally on an oldies station in my dad's car).

This chapter is dedicated to making the time you spend using type in Photoshop more productive. Here's the weird thing about Photoshop type—back in version 6, Adobe added most of the high-end typography features found in Adobe's high-end page layout program InDesign. Which made me think, "Why?" I can't imagine setting a book or magazine article in Photoshop, because when Photoshop type gets below 12 points, it starts to get fuzzy, so laying out columns of text and tweaking the balance, spacing, and paragraph specs for columns of type just doesn't make sense. Then I figured out what's going on. Somebody at Adobe must be hittin' the crack pipe. Could that be it? Or is it so not, that it freaks you out.

TYPE CHANGES, NO PROBLEM

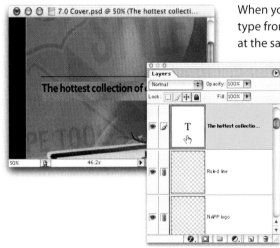

When you want to automatically highlight the type from a Type layer and switch to the Type tool at the same time to make some copy changes, just double-click directly on the "T" icon in the Layers palette, next to the Type layer you want to edit, and blam!, you're ready to go.

RENDERING TEXT IN JUST ONE CLICK

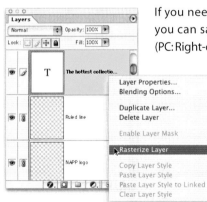

If you need to convert your Type layer into an image layer, you can save some time by simply holding the Control key (PC: Right-click) and clicking directly on the Type layer name that appears in the Layers palette. A pop-up menu will appear where you can choose Rasterize Layer to instantly render your type.

MADE TO FIT

To create a "text box" for your type to fit within, select the Type tool, then click-and-drag out the area you want for your text box. Your type will now fit within that box. When you're finished entering your text, just press Enter to get out of the text bounding box.

TEXT-PATH-MAKING MANIAC

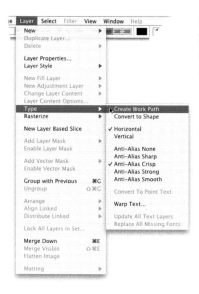

If you want to convert your Type layer into paths (as if you meticulously drew the type with the Pen tool—your clients won't have to know), simply go under the Layer menu, under Type, and choose Create Work Path.

⚫ ⚫ ⚫ **PICTURE THIS: PUTTING A PHOTO INSIDE TYPE**

First, set your Foreground color to black (by pressing "d"). Choose the Type tool and create your text (you don't have to rasterize the type). Then, open the image you want to appear inside your type and drag it into your type document (it should appear on the layer above your Type layer. If it doesn't, just go to the Layers palette and move it on top of your Type layer). To put your image inside the type, press Command-G (PC: Control-G) and whammo—your image is masked into your type. You can reposition the image by using the Move tool. And since you didn't rasterize your Type layer, your text remains totally editable—just click on the Type layer and start editing. You can add Layer Styles to your Type layer to further enhance the effect. If you're not crazy about the image you picked, press Shift-Command-G (PC: Shift-Control-G) to remove the image.

FONTS, FONTS, AND MORE FONTS

Here's a tip to quickly change typefaces and see the change while you make it. First, highlight the type you want to change, and then press Command-H (PC: Control-H) to hide the highlighting (the type is still highlighted, the highlight is just hidden from view). Then, up in the Options Bar, click once in the font field, then use the Up/Down Arrow keys on your keyboard to scroll through your installed typefaces. Man, do I love this one.

MAKE YOUR TEXT JUMP INTO ACTION

Earlier, I gave you the quick tip for rasterizing your type by Control-clicking (PC: Right-clicking) on your Type layer, then choosing Rasterize Layer from the pop-up menu that appears. Believe it or not, there's an even faster way, if you don't mind spending a minute or two up front setting it up. Create an action that rasterizes the type for you so that you can rasterize anytime with just one key. Here's how: Create a Type layer, then make the Actions palette visible. Choose New Action from the Actions palette pull-down menu (the circle with the right-facing arrow in it). Name your new action "Rasterize Type Layer," then, from the F-key pop-up menu choose and assign an F-key to this action. Click the Record button (it's where the OK button usually is), then go under the Layer menu, under Type, and choose Rasterize. Now go back to the Actions palette and click on the Stop button at the bottom of the palette (it's the first button from the left). That's it, your action is written. Test it by creating a Type layer, then pressing the F-key you assigned to your action. It should instantly rasterize (you'll know if it worked, because the "T" icon on the Type layer will no longer be visible).

DOUBLE YOUR PLEASURE

We've already talked about rasterizing text, but once you've rasterized your Type layer into a regular image layer, your type is no longer editable (meaning you can't go back and change type faces, type in a different word, adjust leading or kerning, etc.). Here's a quick way around that limitation. Before rasterizing (rendering) your type, duplicate the Type layer by dragging it to the New Layer icon at the bottom of the Layers palette. Then, hide the original Type layer from view (by clicking on the Eye icon next to the original Type layer). That way, if you ever need to go back and change the word (or font, leading, etc.), you have the original editable Type layer still available. Just simply make it visible.

SEEING YOUR TYPE CHANGE COLOR

Have you noticed that when you highlight your text to change the color, the highlighting completely covers your type. So what's the big deal? While it's highlighted, you can't see what the colored type looks like until you click off the type. Here's a tip that lets you see the type as you colorize it: After you highlight your type, press Command-H (PC: Control-H), the shortcut for hiding Extras.

MOVE YOUR TYPE, WITHOUT SWITCHING TOOLS

Here's a tip that can save you a lot of tool switching when formatting your type. Once you create your type, if you need to move it, you don't have to switch to the Move tool—just move your Type cursor away from your type (either above, below, or an inch or so to the right or left), and your cursor will temporarily change to the Move tool. You can now simply click-and-drag your type. If you want to edit your type some more, just move your cursor near the type again.

EDITING TEXT BY HIGHLIGHTING IT

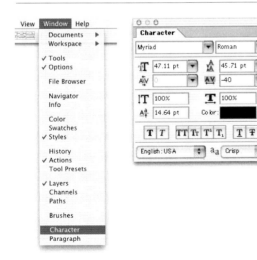

Here's a cool little tip for changing your font size without having the Type tool active. Just click on your Type layer (in the Layers palette), then go under the Window menu and choose Character. When the Character palette appears, you can make changes to your type size, color, font, tracking, etc. It freaks you out, doesn't it?

RASTERIZE TIMES 2, 4, 6...

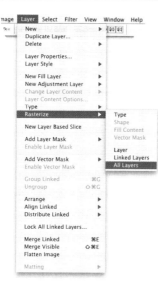

If you have multiple Type layers and you want to convert them all to image layers, there's a way to do it without individually rasterizing each. Simply go under the Layer menu, under Rasterize, and choose All Layers. This will rasterize all the Type layers at once.

HONEY, I NEED SOME SPACE: VISUALLY ADJUST KERNING

You can visually control the spacing between your type (which is much better than numerically trying to figure it out) by using the same keyboard shortcuts for adjusting type that Adobe Illustrator uses. Here's how: To set the tracking tighter (tightening the space between a group of letters or words), highlight the type then press Option-Left Arrow (PC: Alt-Left Arrow) to tighten. Press Option-Right Arrow (PC: Alt-Right Arrow) to add more space between a selected group of letters or words. To adjust the space between two individual letters (called kerning) click your cursor between the two letters and use the same keyboard shortcuts mentioned above.

TELL PHOTOSHOP WHEN YOU'RE DONE WITH TYPE

As you probably know, you can jump to most any tool in the Toolbox by pressing a single-key keyboard shortcut. (If you didn't know that, sell your copy of Photoshop. Kidding. Just turn to Chapter 2 for some essential tips.) Here's the problem: While creating type with the Type tool, if you press one of those one-key shortcuts (let's say the letter "p" for the Pen tool), instead of jumping to the Pen tool, Photoshop types the letter "p". It'll drive you nuts. Okay, you won't go nuts, but at the very least you'll have a lot of typos. The reason is this: You have to tell Photoshop that you're done editing your type. You do this in one of three ways: (1) click on the check icon at the far right of the Options Bar, (2) press the Enter key, or (3) switch to another tool manually by clicking on it in the Toolbox. Any of these three tells Photoshop that you're done and lets you use the single-key shortcuts to switch tools.

BRING THOSE TYPE LAYERS TOGETHER

How do you merge two Type layers together? Unfortunately, while they're still editable Type layers, you can't—you have to rasterize the layers first. Technically, you rasterize just one (the bottom of the two Type layers), and then make the top Type layer active and press Command-E (PC: Control-E) to merge these two layers together. However, when you do that, the top Type layer will automatically rasterize as the two layers are combined into one, so there's really no way around it—with the exception of this little tip: Highlight the editable type on the top layer and choose Cut from the Edit menu. Switch to the lower Type layer, click your Type cursor once at the end of the type, press Return (PC: Enter) to start a new line, then choose Paste from the Edit menu to paste the contents of the top Type layer into the bottom Type layer. Then drag the old top Type layer into the Trash icon at the bottom of the Layers palette. Although it takes a little effort, now you have both layers combined into one layer (your goal), but the type remains totally editable (the bonus).

THE LONG AND THE SHORT OF TYPE

Although the Character palette has numeric controls for making your type fatter (horizontal scaling) or taller (vertical scaling), it's usually easier to do these two functions visually (rather than numerically). Here's how: First set your type, then switch to the Move tool. Press Command-T (PC: Control-T) to bring up the Free Transform bounding box. To make your type fatter, grab the center handle on either side and drag outward. To make your type taller, grab the center handle on the top and drag upward, or on the bottom and drag downward.

MADE TO FIT: PART TWO

This tip relates to a previous tip, where you created what's called a "text box" so that your type wraps within a text block, rather than running in one straight line. The tip is this: If you've created some standard type by just clicking and typing rather than creating a paragraph text block, you're not out of luck. While the Type layer is active, just go under the Layer menu, under Type, and choose Convert to Paragraph Text. Now your type will wrap within the text box boundaries, and you can edit the boundaries by adjusting the corner and center points.

TYPE MASK FUNCTION: IT'S NOT JUST FOR BREAKFAST ANYMORE

You'll probably come across situations where you'll need a selection in the shape of type, rather than the solid type itself. Adobe knew this, and that's why they created the Type Mask function. (Note: In versions prior to Photoshop 6.0, it used to be a tool, but in Photoshop 6.0 it was a type option in the Options Bar. Now it's a tool again in 7.0.) To turn this function on, just click-and-hold on the Type tool and choose the Horizontal Type Mask tool from the flyout menu. When you click this Type tool within your image window, a red tint will appear over your image, and as you type, your text will appear in the red tint. Edit the type as you would any type, and when you switch to another tool, the red tint goes away, and your type becomes a selection. However, here's a tip for a different method that we actually prefer, which provides the same end result. Just use your regular Type tool and set your type just like you always would. When it looks right, Command-click (PC: Right-click) on your Type layer's name in the Layers palette to put a selection around it. Then drag your Type layer into the Trash icon at the bottom of the Layers palette, and voilà, there's your selection in the exact shape of your type.

T	Horizontal Type Tool	T
T	Vertical Type Tool	T
	Horizontal Type Mask Tool	T
	Vertical Type Mask Tool	T

● ● ● EXACT SIZING FOR YOUR TEXT COLUMNS

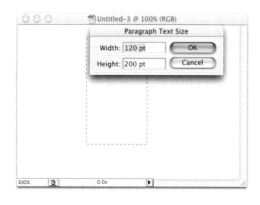

We already showed you how to create a column of type by clicking and dragging the Type tool to create your "text box" so your text will wrap within that column. But here's a quick little tip that lets you tell Photoshop exactly the Width and Height you'd like your type column to be (rather than just clicking and dragging it out visually). With the Type tool, just hold the Option key (PC: Alt key) and click in your document and the Paragraph Text Size dialog box will appear where you can enter the exact size you'd like for your column.

● ● ● REMOVING THOSE TYPOGRAPHICALLY INCORRECT SPACES

If you're trying to set type that looks "typographically" correct in Photoshop, there's an old habit you'll have to break, and that's the curse of putting two spaces at the end of every sentence. This is a holdover from people who at one time used traditional typewriters, where adding two spaces was necessary, but in "typesetting" that's a huge no-no. About 70% of the text I copy and paste from text files that people give me has two spaces, but I use this Photoshop 7.0 tip to fix the problem in just seconds. First, highlight your paragraph of type. Then, go under the Edit menu and choose Find and Replace Text. In the Find What field, press the Spacebar twice (entering two spaces), then in Change To, press the Spacebar just once. Click Change All, and every time Photoshop finds two spaces at the end of a sentence, it will replace it with just one, making you typographically correct.

TWEAK ALL YOUR TYPE WITH ONE FELL SWOOP!

This is a pretty darn slick tip for changing the font, size, or color of a number of different Type layers all at once. Here's how it's done: First, link all the layers that you want to adjust by clicking in the second column beside each Type layer. Once all the layers are linked, hold the Shift key and make your change. The change you make to one Type layer will also affect all the linked Type layers. The key is *not to* highlight your type. Just choose the Type tool and go straight to the Options Bar or the Character palette. Schweeeet!

DON'T HAVE ITALIC OR BOLD? DON'T SWEAT IT

If you have a typeface that doesn't have a bold or italic version available, don't sweat it— Photoshop can make a fake bold or italic version for you. They're called faux bold and faux italic (don't pronounce them "fox bold" or the French will get really cranky about it. It's pronounced "fo," as in "Fe, Fi, Fo, Fum"). To apply a faux style to the type, highlight your type and choose Faux Bold or Faux Italic from the Character palette's pop-down menu. Here's another tip: Don't forget to turn off these faux styles when you're done, because they don't automatically turn themselves off. Vive le Français!

I NEED MY DUMB QUOTES AGAIN

In all previous versions of Photoshop, when you typed in a quote mark (") or apostrophe ('), what Photoshop gave you was the typographically incorrect inch mark (") or foot mark (') instead. They're called "dumb quotes." Luckily, in Photoshop 7.0, Adobe brought these typographically challenged dummies into line, and now they're properly applied as "curly quotes" by default, which is great. That is unless you have to actually type an inch mark or a foot mark. Here's the workaround—when it comes time to type in an inch or foot mark, go under the Photoshop menu, under Preferences, and choose General Preferences (in Windows and Mac OS 9.x, Preferences can be found under the Edit menu). In the General Preferences dialog box, turn off Use Smart Quotes, and then type in your characters. When you're done, return to the General Preferences and turn them back on to bring typographic order to your world.

MAKING THE SPELL CHECKER OBEY YOUR COMMANDS

7.0's spell checker isn't just window dressing, it has a very robust spell-checking function, akin to Adobe InDesign's own spell checker, but if you understand how it works, you can save yourself some time and frustration. Basically, if you highlight some text on a layer, it checks just the highlighted text, so if you highlight one word, it just checks that one word (even if there are dozens of words in your paragraph). If you choose to spell check but don't have anything highlighted, it checks

your entire document, regardless of how many Type layers you have. It's also helpful to know that it only checks real Type layers (layers that have a capital "T" as their thumbnail image in the Layers palette), and it cannot spell check any layers with text that have been rasterized (converted from a Type layer into a regular image layer).

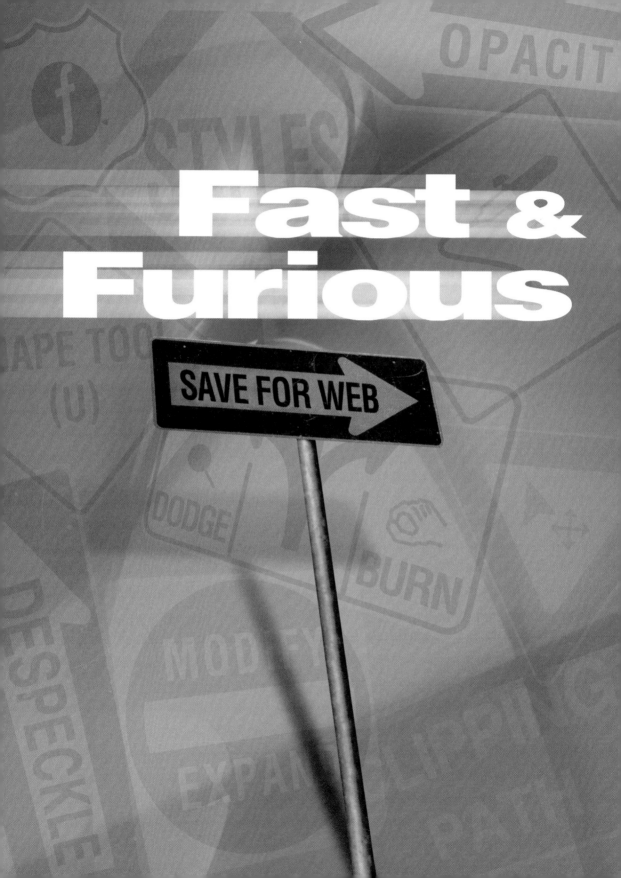

The reason I call this chapter "Killer Web Tips" is because most of the tips in this chapter came from a buddy of mine who's now serving time in Rayford

Fast & Furious
killer web tips

State Penitentiary for manslaughter. Technically, he's not really a killer, and technically this chapter should have been called "Web Tips From a Killer" rather than "Killer Web Tips," but really, would you have bought this book if that was the name of this chapter? You would have? Wow! You're my kind of person (or trustee, as my friend likes to call them).

Seriously though, in this chapter we're going to look at some tips to make optimizing your graphics easier and faster, while making your file sizes as small as possible. If you incorporate these tips into your Web work, before you know it, you'll be earning more money, and then when you have enough money, you can buy cartons of cigarettes to bribe the guards. See, it all works out in the end.

◉ ◉ ◉ ZOOM OUT FOR SHARPER WEB IMAGES

This is a tip we use almost daily when we have to greatly reduce the size and/or resolution of an image. Sometimes when you make a drastic size/resolution change, it can really make the resulting image blurry, so what we do is simply zoom out on the image so that the window and image are at either 50% or 25% view. Then, we take a screen capture of our image window at the new smaller size. That way, the image still looks sharp, but it's much smaller when we open the screen capture in Photoshop. The trick to making this work is using either a 50%, 25%, or 12.5% view size for making the capture. If you view the image at 66.7%, 33.3%, or 16.7%, the image won't be as crisp (because of the way Photoshop draws the image at those views).

◉ ◉ ◉ IMAGEREADY FEATURE COMES TO PHOTOSHOP

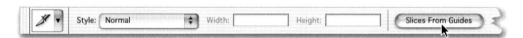

One of our favorite little features from Adobe ImageReady has made its way into Photoshop—it's called "Slices From Guides." What it does is slice your image (for the Web) where your guides are positioned. To make use of this handy little number, just make your rulers visible, drag out guides where you'd like your slices applied, and then switch to the Slice tool (press the letter "k"). Once you've got the Slice tool, look up in the Options Bar and you'll find a button called Slices From Guides. Click the button and Photoshop will do the rest.

TWO EASY WAYS TO CREATE TRANSPARENCY

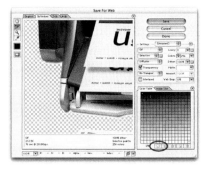

Back in Photoshop 6.0, the most common method for making a background transparent is still available to you in Photoshop 7.0, and that's to go to the Layers palette and simply delete the Background layer. That's it. This leaves only the layers that were above the Background layer (which already have background transparency). Now, in 7.0, there's another easy way, and that's to go to Photoshop's Save for Web command, switch to the Eyedropper tool in the Save for Web's Toolbox, and click on the background color you want to become transparent. Then, just below the Color Table on the bottom right of the dialog, click on the first icon, which creates transparency from your selected color.

NEED TO SHRINK THE FILE SIZE? USE TRANSPARENCY

Want a killer tip for squeezing even more size out of your GIF Web images? Make something transparent. That's right, if you can pick an area of your image to make transparent, your file size will drop like a rock. For example, if you're putting a logo over a white background and you can make the white area around the logo transparent, your file size will be significantly smaller, because the transparent areas are virtually ignored when determining file size, because, after all, there's nothing there.

IF IT'S WEB SAFE, DON'T USE IT

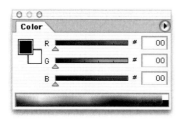

The one Color palette that we absolutely don't use at all anymore is the Web-safe Color palette. Why? You don't need it—and it can make your file sizes significantly larger than necessary. The Web-safe colors were created back when most computer users had computers that could only display a maximum of 256 colors. Out of those 256, the "Web-safe" colors were the 216 colors that were the same on both Macintosh and Windows browsers. Even back then you could still use a non-Web-safe color, but it might dither to the next closest Web-safe color so the color might be off a bit. However, if you've ever looked at a row of monitors at the computer store, you'll notice the color is slightly different on every one, but that's another story. Luckily these days, you'd be hard-pressed to find anyone using such a lame computer that it only displays 256 colors. They haven't sold a computer like that for literally years.

CHANGE ONE PREFERENCE, SAVE A BUNDLE

If you're creating Web graphics with Photoshop and you're *not* using the Save for Web feature (which is perfectly fine not to do), make sure you go under the Photoshop menu (in Mac OS X), under Preferences, and choose File Handling (in Windows and Mac OS 9.x, Preferences can be found under the Edit menu). In the Image Previews pop-up, change the setting from Always Save to Never Save. Image Previews are those tiny thumbnail icons that are visible on your system. They look cute, but they take up big space—often accounting for 70% of your file size. Turn them off, and you'll save file size big time. (Save for Web does this automatically, so if you're using that feature, don't sweat it.)

GET THE REAL 100% VIEW

Image Size

Pixel Dimensions: 229K (was 637K)

Width: `60.03` percent

Height: `60|` percent

OK
Cancel
Auto...

Document Size:

Width: `5.233` inches

Height: `2.883` inches

Resolution: `72` pixels/inch

☑ Constrain Proportions
☑ Resample Image: Bicubic

When creating Web graphics, it's often important to view your graphic at the same size your audience will view it. To view your image at 100%, just double-click on the Zoom tool. If your image is too big when viewed at 100%, just zoom out until the view of your image is the size you'd like it to appear on the Web page (use the zoom-out shortcuts—Zoom tool holding the Option/Alt keys, etc.), then look in the lower-left corner of the image window and you'll see the percentage of zoom. Write that down, then go under the Image menu and choose Image Size. When the Image Size dialog box appears, in the Height pop-up menu in the Pixel Dimensions section, choose Percent. Then enter the percentage amount you wrote down earlier. By default, Photoshop will enter the Width when you enter the Height setting to keep your image proportional (if not, make sure the Constrain Proportions checkbox is turned on at the bottom). Click OK and it resizes your image to the exact size you want it to appear on the Web page.

LET PHOTOSHOP MAKE THE FILE SIZE CALL

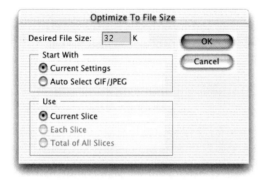

Oftentimes you have a target size you're trying to hit when creating Web graphics (for example, you're creating a Web banner and your file size limit is 32 K). If that's the case, and you know the target size, why not let Photoshop do all the work? Here's how: Under the File menu, go to Save for Web. In the Save for Web dialog box, just to the right of the Settings pop-up menu, is a right-facing triangle. Click-and-hold on it, and when the pop-up menu appears, choose Optimize to File Size. In the dialog box, enter the target file size you need your graphic to be and click OK to have Photoshop optimize the graphic to fit your target file size. If it doesn't matter to you whether it's a GIF or JPEG, choose Auto Select GIF/JPEG and Photoshop will "make the call."

LET PHOTOSHOP WRITE THE CODE TOO!

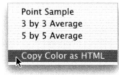

As you may know, there are hexadecimal codes for the colors used in Web pages. Not only does Photoshop know these hexadecimal codes, it can extract them from an image and let you paste them into your HTML code editor. First, press the letter "i" to switch to the Eyedropper tool, and then hold the Control key (PC: Right-click) and click on a color within your image. A pop-up menu will appear where you can choose Copy Color as HTML. Now you can switch to your HTML editor and choose Paste to copy the HTML code into your app.

GET SUPER-CLEAN TYPE FOR THE WEB

If you've been faced with having to create small type on the Web (usually 12 points or below), you know the smaller you go, the blurrier your type gets. That's because of the anti-aliasing that is automatically applied to the type, which works fine at larger sizes but tends to run together at smaller sizes, making your type look fuzzy. You can adjust the amount of aliasing (from the Options Bar), but here's a tip that many Web designers feel works even better: Once you get below 12 points, start adding positive tracking to your type (anywhere between 20 to 50 points) in the Character palette. This increases the amount of space between letters, and therefore, decreases the amount of blurriness. By increasing the space between your letters in this way, it minimizes the effects of anti-aliasing and makes your type cleaner and more readable at smaller sizes. As a general rule—the smaller the type, the larger the tracking amount.

GOT A FOLDER FULL OF IMAGES FOR THE WEB? BATCH 'EM!

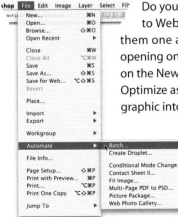

Do you have a whole folder of images that you're going to convert to Web graphics? If the images are somewhat similar, don't do them one at a time—automate the process using Actions. Start by opening one image from the folder. Go to the Actions palette and click on the New Action button. Give this action a name (something like Optimize as JPEGs) then go about the business of optimizing this one graphic into a JPEG for the Web. When you're done optimizing it, click the Stop button at the bottom of the Actions palette. Then go under the File menu, under Automate, and choose Batch. In this dialog, under Play, choose the name of the new action you just created. Under Source, choose the folder of images you want converted using that action, and under Destination, choose what you want to happen to those images after they're converted. Click OK, and Photoshop will convert that folder with absolutely blinding speed. This one tip can really change the way you work, especially if you create for print first, then repurpose for the Web afterward.

CHAPTER 5 • Killer Web Tips   **99**

FILE-NAMING TIMESAVER FOR MAC USERS

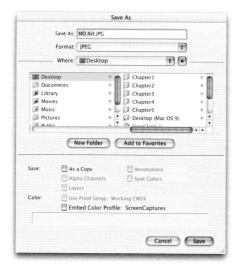

This particular tip is really more for Macintosh users because Mac users don't have to add file name extensions to their files, unless they're creating Web graphics. Because of that reason, many Mac users disable Photoshop's preference that automatically adds a file name extension to their files. Even though that's the case, when Mac users are creating Web graphics, it's important to include the .gif or .jpg file names, but the good news is—you don't have to turn on the auto file extension feature—just hold the Option key as you choose your file format from the Save As dialog box, and Photoshop will then add the appropriate .gif or .jpg file extension to your Web graphics files.

READ THE WEB COLOR ONSCREEN

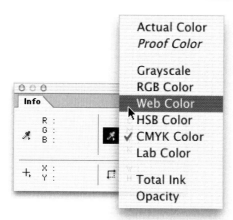

Want to know the hexadecimal Web color values of any color in your image? The Info palette can tell you instantly. Go under the Window menu and choose Show Info. In the Info palette, click on the little Eyedropper icon next to the CMYK readout and a pop-up menu appears. Choose Web Color, and you'll get the hexadecimal readouts right in the palette.

CROP IT EVEN CLOSER

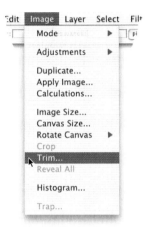

When you're designing graphics for the Web, you don't want even one extra pixel of unused space, because it adds to the overall file size of the image. Because of that, you want to crop your Web graphics as tightly as possible. Luckily for us (you, them, etc.), Photoshop 7.0 can do it for you automatically. Just choose Trim from the Image menu, click OK in the dialog box, and it will crop your Web graphic as tightly as possible for the smallest possible file size. It does this by looking at the pixel color in the upper left-hand corner of your image and cropping down until it hits another color. (Note: The Trim dialog also gives you the option to base the crop on the bottom right-hand corner pixel color or transparent areas). This works especially great when creating type for the Web, because you'll often create it on a white background.

LOSE THOSE ANNOYING NUMBERS IN THE UPPER LEFT-HAND CORNER

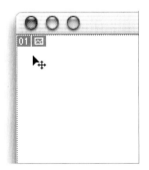

We get more letters from people who ask us, How do I get rid of that number in the top left-hand corner of my image?" This little puppy appears if you accidentally click on the Slice tool in the Toolbox. Even if you notice your error and immediately switch to another tool—it's too late. The "slice number" is already in place. To make it go away, go under the View menu, under Show, and choose Slices. Then try not to accidentally click on the Slice tool again. (Sorry, I just felt like scolding somebody. You know, just for fun.)

MAKE SURE YOU SEE IT THE SAME WAY THEY SEE IT

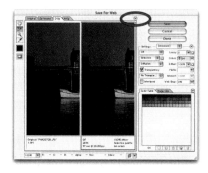

If you're designing Web graphics on a Macintosh, you can be sure they're going to be viewed by lots of people using a PC, and vice versa. A design problem arises because the monitors on Macs and on PCs display with different levels of brightness. For example, if you design Web graphics on a Macintosh, they'll look more than 10% darker when viewed on a PC using Windows. Photoshop will let you see an approximation of how those graphics will look when viewed on a PC. Here's how: Choose Save for Web from the File menu. Then, at the top right of the preview window is a pop-up menu called the Preview Menu. From that menu, choose Standard Windows Color to get a preview of how your currently opened graphic will look when viewed on a standard Windows monitor. Window designers can do the same thing and view how their Web graphics will look when viewed on a Mac (they'll look lighter). Knowing how your graphics will look on each platform will help you find a happy middle ground that looks good on both.

DON'T LOAD THAT BOGUS SLICE!

If you're slicing images for the Web in Photoshop (using the Slice tool), here's a tip to save even more space. If you have a slice in your image that's going to be the same color as your background (for example, you've got a solid white slice going on a solid white background), you can save file size by having that slice load no image at all. Sound like a plan? (I thought you'd like that.) Here's how to do it: Once your slice is in place, make it active (using the Slice Select tool), and then click on the Slice Options button in the Options Bar. A dialog box will appear, and in the Slice Type pop-up menu, choose No Image and click OK. That way, when Photoshop generates its HTML for the page, there will be no image in that spot, just the white background showing through, giving you a faster loading Web page. Pretty sweet!

USE LAYER-BASED SLICES

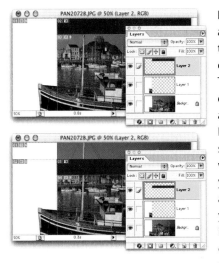

If you're getting ready to slice an image for the Web and you still have your layers intact—don't flatten that image before you slice. Instead, let Photoshop create the slices for you (called layer-based slices). There are two main advantages: (1) it's easier. You don't have to drag out slices—Photoshop does it automatically, perfectly slicing at the size of your layer. But even better is (2), when you create a layer-based slice, you can move the layer and (get this) Photoshop will automatically adjust all the slices to accommodate your move, and it will create a new slice for your layer as well. If you slice manually and move your layer—you're out of luck—the old slice stays right where it was. Plus, creating a layer-based slice couldn't be easier. Click on the layer you want to slice, then go under the Layer menu and choose New Layer Based Slice—Photoshop does the rest.

BLUR THAT JPEG AND SHRINK IT DOWN

Here's a cool tip for when you're creating JPEG images. This tip doesn't work for all images, but can really come in handy for others. The tip is this: If you can slightly blur your image, because of the way JPEG compression works, the file size will be smaller. You could just add a Gaussian Blur, or you could blur the image directly from the Save for Web dialog box by entering a number in the Blur field. However, you're usually better off putting a selection around the important areas of your image, then inverting the selection and blurring just the background. That way, the important parts stay sharp, and the noncritical areas become more compressed.

IMAGEREADY WINDOW SPEED TIP

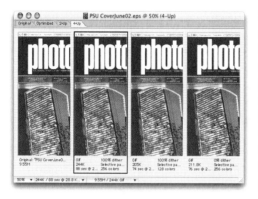

If you're using Adobe ImageReady (which comes installed with Photoshop as part of the package), by default the image window displays the original (unoptimized version) of your image. However, if you want to quickly view the optimized version, a 2-Up version (original and optimized side by side), or the 4-Up version (your original and three other optimized options), you can use the quick tip Command-Y (PC: Control-Y) to rotate through your four view choices. A big timesaver.

SPEND MORE TIME ANIMATING, LESS TIME CLICKING

If you're building Web animations in ImageReady, you don't have to keep clicking the tiny controls at the bottom of the Animations palette. Instead, navigate using these quick shortcuts: To play your animation, press Shift-Spacebar. To stop it, press Shift-Spacebar again. Press Option-Left Arrow (PC: Alt-Left Arrow) to go to the previous frame. Press Option-Right Arrow (PC: Alt-Right Arrow) to go to the next frame. To quickly jump back to the beginning of your animation, press Shift-Option-Left Arrow (PC: Shift-Alt-Left Arrow).

IMAGEREADY'S SUPERCHARGED EYEDROPPER

In previous versions of Photoshop, you could only use the Eyedropper tool to sample a color from other open images in Photoshop, but for some reason, ImageReady had a supercharged Eyedropper. If you held the mouse button down, you could leave your image window and sample colors from, well… just about anything—including your computer desktop or any other open application. Freaky! Fortunately, Adobe finally added this same power to Photoshop 7.0's Eyedropper tool.

IMAGEREADY'S AUTO TILE MAKER

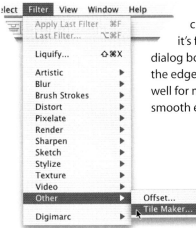

ImageReady has a built-in seamless tile creator for creating seamless backgrounds. It's called Tile Maker and it's found under the Filter menu, under Other. It brings up a dialog box where you can choose how much you want to blend the edges of your images (the default setting of 10 works fairly well for most images), but you can increase it if it doesn't look smooth enough to you.

EXERCISING YOUR INFLUENCE ON GIFS

Indexed Color

Palette: Local (Selective)

Colors: 256

Forced: Black and White

☑ Transparency

OK

Cancel

☑ Preview

Options

Matte: None

Dither: Diffusion

Amount: 75 %

☐ Preserve Exact Colors

This is an old trick we use to influence how Photoshop builds its color table when creating GIF images. We put a selection around the area of the image that's most important to us (for example, if we had a product shot, we'd put a selection around it), then we'd convert to Index Color. Photoshop will look at the colors contained in your selection and build the Indexed Color Table giving preference to those colors. It's another slick way to use less colors, creating a smaller file, but with a better-looking image.

STYLE WARNING FOR WEB DESIGNERS

New Style

☑ Name: MyCustomStyles

☑ Include Layer Effects

☑ Include Layer Blending Options

OK

Cancel

If you're designing Web graphics using Photoshop and ImageReady, you're probably spending a decent amount of time swapping back and forth between the two apps. Although the two programs share many of the same features and commands, one thing they don't share is custom Styles that you've saved in Photoshop's Styles palette. So just be forewarned, if you create a custom style in Photoshop, don't expect to find that same style in ImageReady.

As I'm sure you've noticed by now, this book is filled with Photoshop topic-specific tips, such as layers tips or production tips, but there's a whole

Fast Company
photoshop design tips

subset of tips that aren't as much about pressing a keyboard shortcut or a hidden command, as they are about what we've learned while working in our studio on real-world projects.

Unfortunately, the studio we work in is a hair studio, so many of our tips are like, "Use Paul Mitchell products" or "Lather, rinse, and repeat," so I'm not sure how helpful they'll be, but I guarantee you this—you'll have shiny, more manageable hair in just two weeks.

Okay, they're actually Photoshop tips, but they answer questions that are much more broad, such as "How far is the drop shadow supposed to be from an object?", "How do I scan a 3-dimensional object?", or "How much conditioner should I use for a dry oily scalp?" Did you catch that "dry oily" oxymoron? You didn't? I'm not sure you're ready for these tips. Apply a cream rinse, then we'll talk.

⬤ ⬤ ⬤ FOCUSING ATTENTION USING COLOR

You've seen this effect done over and over again, most recently by a slew of Gatorade® commercials. Here's a quick technique to achieve this effect. Open an image. Press Shift-Command-U (PC: Shift-Control-U) to Desaturate the image. Choose the History Brush from the Toolbox. Open the History palette and click on the column to the left of the History State that says "Open." Now simply paint back in the areas you wish to remain full color.

⬤ ⬤ ⬤ FOCUSING ATTENTION BY ADDING DEPTH

Here's a trick for defining depth to the viewer of your artwork: Make the objects that are farther away appear out of focus or blurry, and make the objects that are near, sharp and crisp. You can use this technique for drawing attention to objects in the foreground of your Photoshop image by slightly blurring the background of your image. This adds depth and dimension to your artwork, as well as focusing attention. To do this, put a selection around the area you want the focus on, add a 10-pixel Feather, Inverse the selection (from the Select menu), then apply your Blur.

SHADOW OPACITY AND SOFTNESS

The softness (or blurriness) and the opacity (or transparency) of a shadow depends on how close the object casting the shadow is to the background or object that it's casting the shadow onto. The rule to follow is this: The farther away the object, the softer and less opaque the shadow will be (see example on left). Take a look at the settings we used in the Layer Style/Drop Shadow dialog box. The Opacity was lowered to 30% to make it more transparent. The Distance is 35 pixels so that the floating type looks farther away from the background, and the Size (softness or blur) is set to 15 pixels to give it a soft (blurry) edge. Together, this gives the text the appearance of being higher, or farther away from the background.

Now the closer the object, the shadow will have harder edges and be more opaque (see example on left).

Once again, look at the settings we used to create our shadow. This time we made the shadow more opaque by raising the Opacity to 50%, and we lowered both the Distance and the Size. Without ever moving our text, we made our type look closer to the background just by changing the softness, and opacity of the drop shadow.

OVERLAP GRAPHIC ELEMENTS TO ADD VISUAL INTEREST

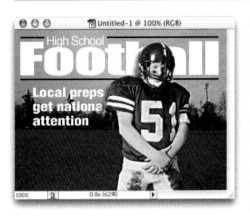

A great way to add visual interest to any design project is to overlap an image over text. This simple technique will add depth to your design project, giving even a simple newsletter or masthead a more dramatic visual impact.

First, place your text or nameplate over a background image. Now, go back to the background image in the Layers palette and select the areas you want to overlap the text (using the selection tool of your choice). Place this selection on its own layer by pressing Command-J (PC: Control-J), then move it to the top of the Layers palette above your text or nameplate layer. It's that simple.

USE CORRECT CMYK BUILDS TO MATCH PANTONE COLORS

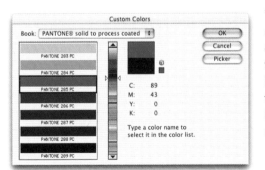

You're working on a Photoshop project, and you want to match a specific Pantone color build. Find the CMYK formula (for the specific Pantone color) from a current Pantone color formula guide, and use that to build your color in Photoshop. Photoshop's CMYK color simulation may not match the printed color standard.

ADD COLOR TO YOUR SHADOWS

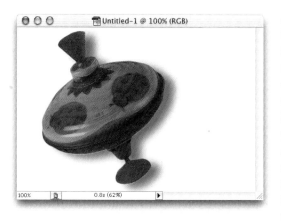

Adding color to a shadow is a quick way to give any layout a nice design twist. Matching the shadow to a surrounding color or other graphic element is a great way to tie the layout together. Here's the quick way first: Isolate the object from the background with the selection tool of your choice (if you pasted an image into a new document, it will already be in a separate layer), and Press Command-J (PC: Control-J) to place the selection on its own layer. Click on the Add a Layer Style icon (the black circle with the little "ƒ" in it) and choose Drop Shadow. Click on the Color Swatch and select a color from your image by moving your cursor over the image (your cursor will turn into an Eyedropper) and clicking on the color. You can edit the shadow settings to achieve the desired results. If you want to put another artsy twist on it (and we do), make a custom shadow with the Gradient tool and use Free Transform to add some perspective.

PICKING COLORS? USE THE BUILT-IN COLOR WHEEL

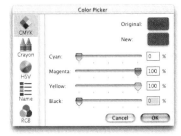

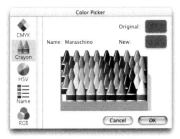

If you need some help in picking complementary colors for your Photoshop artwork, you can request a different Color Picker (one that looks more like a traditional color wheel), rather than using Photoshop's standard Color Picker (which isn't much help at all). This is done in the Photoshop menu (in Mac OS X), under General Preferences (in Windows and Mac OS 9.x, the Preferences can be found under the Edit menu). At the top of the General Prefs' dialog box, you'll see a pop-up menu for Color Picker. By default, it's set to Adobe. If you're using Windows, you can switch it to the standard Windows' Color Picker. If you're on a Macintosh, you can choose to use Apple's Color Picker (actually, there's a host of different Color Pickers on the Mac, including CMYK, RGB, Crayon, and HSV). Apple's HSV Picker gives you a visual color wheel that makes picking complementary colors a breeze.

COLOR COMBINATIONS AFFECT SIZE AND PROPORTION

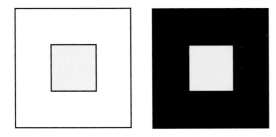

One thing to keep in mind when choosing color combinations is how different colors, and the balance between the colors themselves, affect how we perceive them. For example: Take a yellow square and place it over a white background. Now, take the same size square and place it over a black background. The square on the black background will appear to be smaller, even though the squares are exactly the same size. It's just how we perceive the color combination together. Remember that darker colors tend to look heavier and may overpower lighter colors. Along the same lines, when you place white text or reverse text over a black background, the text appears bold. It's one of those funky eyes-playing-tricks-on-you sort of things.

USE TIGHT CROPPING TO SPICE UP IMAGES

We've all had those times when we're given less-than-spectacular photographic images to work with. It's your client's son or daughter, or maybe a really bad snapshot of a boring showroom or storefront. Here's a quick tip to give unimpressive photos a cool, hip new look: Simply use the Crop tool to tightly crop the image. You may even try rotating the image slightly, to give it that hip look. I know, it's really a no-brainer, but it does add a little pizzaz to boring images.

DETERMINING THE LENGTH OF A CAST SHADOW

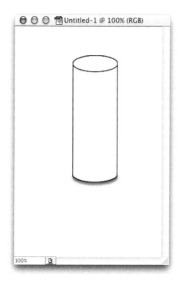

One of the most commonly asked questions about cast shadows is, "How long or short do I make them?" We could get into a long and involved explanation, describing different lighting situations, such as single or multiple light sources, and viewing the subject from a bird's-eye perspective, bla, bla, bla… but we won't get into all that. After all, this is a quick tips book, so we'll oversimplify the answer just a bit.

What it comes down to is this: The length of the shadow is determined by the vertical position of the light source. For example, if the light source is directly above an object, it would hardly cast any shadow at all (see the illustration upper left), but if it was closer to the horizon line, it would cast a longer shadow (see the illustration bottom left).

In layman's terms: the higher the light source, the shorter the shadow; the lower the light source, the longer the shadow.

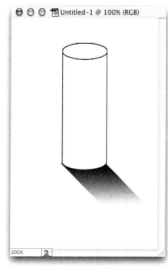

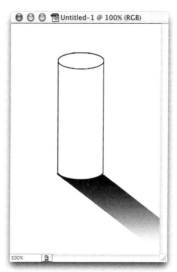

TWO-COLOR MAY BE BETTER THAN FOUR

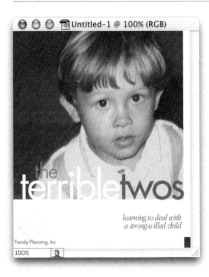

Sometimes we get so obsessed with the four-color process that we forget that we can oftentimes convey the same visual message with two colors. Photoshop gives us amazing control over duotones. Combine that with good use of tints and screens and we can achieve some amazing effects. Not only that, but your clients will fall head over heels for you when they realize that you just saved them some fat dinero.

DON'T MAKE IT BLACK—MAKE IT MEGA BLACK!

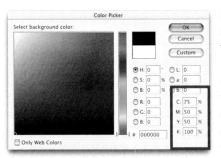

If you're creating a black background for something that will appear in print, don't just fill the background with 100% black. For that rich-looking, deep black, you need to have a custom black build (we call it mega black) for that "midnight black" effect when printed. Our favorite black build is C=75, M=50, Y=50, and K=100. Most traditional print houses use what they call a cyan kicker in their blacks, which is a black color build using 75% cyan and 100% black, but we feel our mega black build is much, well… blacker! Give it a try and see if you agree.

EFFECTIVE GHOSTING OR BACKSCREENING

Ghosting, or backscreening, a photographic image is another very effective design technique. This is a fantastic way to isolate text, logos, or other graphic elements into a photographic image. Simply choose the areas you wish to ghost, or screen (using the selection tool of your choice). Bring up the Levels dialog box, and move the midtone Input Levels adjustment slider (the one in the center) toward the left. Note: When placing text over a ghosted area, be sure to lighten it enough so that your text will be legible.

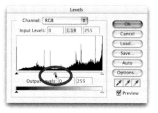

CREATE YOUR OWN CUSTOM TYPEFACE

Photoshop's Type tool gives us the flexibility to customize our fonts by converting the font to paths or selections. In the past, we'd have to customize the fonts in other vector-based applications and then import them into our Photoshop file. Forget that, here's a better way: Open a new Photoshop file and type in some text using the Type tool.

Go under Layer, under Type, and choose Convert to Shape. Now, use the Direct Selection tool to select individual points, and move them wherever you want (as you move the points your layer shape automatically fills in). It's that easy.

ADD A POINT OF REFERENCE TO CONVEY SIZE

If you're using Photoshop to "fool the eye," here are two tips for making objects look dramatically larger than they really are. First, to convey a sense of size, the eye needs a point of reference. So, if you want to create some type that looks 50 feet tall, place a silhouette of a person (just the person, no background) beside the type, and use Free Transform to shrink him to less than 30% of the height of the type.

The second tip is to rasterize your type, then use Free Transform to add a perspective effect to make your type appear as though it is so tall that you (the person viewing the image) are looking up at it (called foreshortening). To add perspective using Free Transform,

first press Command-T (PC: Control-T) to bring up Free Transform. Then, Control-click (PC: Right-click) within the bounding box and a pop-up menu of transformations will appear. Choose Perspective from this list, then grab the upper right-hand corner point and drag inward to create the perspective. When it looks about right to you, press Return (PC: Enter) to lock in your transformation.

I know I'm supposed to write something compelling to make you want to read this chapter, but honestly, they're layer tips. Not that they're

Speedy Gonzalez
layer tips

unimportant—they totally are. But when you say it—"layer tips"—it just doesn't have enough oomph! This chapter name needs more oomph! By the way, as an aside, if you look up the word "oomph" in the 2001 Webster's Abridged Dictionary, Oxford Version, for the actual definition, it's "A bulkiness or powerful quality that is brought on by most chapter heads, with the notable exception of 'Layer Tips'." Hey, I'm not making this stuff up. Those Webster guys are serious (especially the one who had his own show and was friends with Michael Jackson).

⬤ ⬤ ⬤ MISSING YOUR BACKGROUND LAYER? HERE'S THE FIX

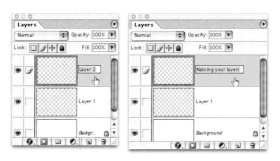

If you're opening new documents and they don't have a Background layer, there's a reason (of course there's a reason, everything has a reason; we just happen to know what it is). The reason is that you've selected the Transparent option in the New document dialog box. That seems like a reasonable thing to do; everybody wants transparency, right? However, what it tells Photoshop is "don't worry about creating a Background layer." To get Background layers again, the next time you're in the New dialog box, under Contents, make sure you choose White, and from then on, you'll have Background layers in your documents.

⬤ ⬤ ⬤ NAMING LAYERS (AND WHY YOU SHOULD)

Okay, admit it. You too have created a multi-layered document (you know, the one with one million layers), and you can't keep track of what was on which layer. A great habit to pick up is to name your layers as you go. To name a new layer as you create it, hold the Option key (PC: Alt key) before you click on the New Layer icon at the bottom of the Layers palette. If you want to rename your layers after you create them, double-click directly on the layer's name in the Layers palette and it will highlight the text so you can type a new name (if you double-click anywhere else besides the name it will bring up the Blending Options in the Layer Style dialog). This way of naming layers directly in the palette is new in Photoshop 7.0. In version 6, you had to hold the Option (PC: Alt) key when you double-clicked and it would bring up the Layer Properties dialog were you could rename the layer. This minor change is a big timesaver.

LOCK ALL THOSE LAYERS IN JUST ONE CLICK

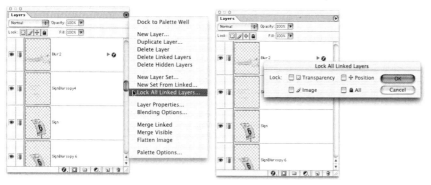

You can lock all of your linked layers at once by choosing Lock All Linked Layers from the Layers palette's pop-down menu. They'll kick and scratch for a while, but they'll eventually calm right down.

TOGGLE THROUGH THE BLEND MODES

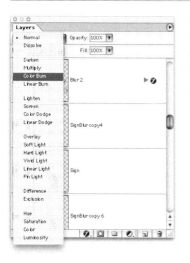

When I'm struggling to get just the right effect by changing the layer Blend Modes, it's great to be able to rotate through each mode without having to go back to the Blend Mode pop-down menu every time. To do this, simply press Shift-+ (plus sign). Every time you press it, it goes to the next Blend Mode.

HIDE YOUR OTHER LAYERS IN THE BLINK OF AN EYE

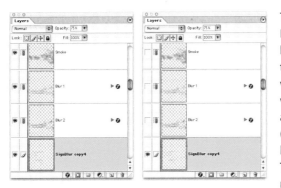

To hide an individual layer, click on the Eye icon in the first column next to that layer in the Layers palette. To make the layer visible again, click on the spot where the Eye icon used to be. If you want to keep one layer visible and hide all the others, hold the Option key (PC: Alt key) and click on the Eye icon beside the layer you want to keep visible. To make the other layers visible again, repeat the process.

WHY DRAGGING AND DROPPING STYLES ROCKS!

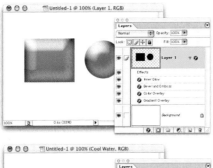

You probably already know that you can apply Styles to an image from the Styles palette, and you may even know that rather than just clicking on them, you can drag-and-drop these styles right from the palette straight onto your current layer. But what's the advantage of dragging and dropping? Isn't it actually harder to drag-and-drop, rather than just clicking once? The advantage is that you can drag-and-drop styles to *any* layer, not just your currently active layer. You can also drag-and-drop effects between different open documents.

⚫ ⚫ ⚫ APPLYING LAYER STYLES TO YOUR BACKGROUND LAYER

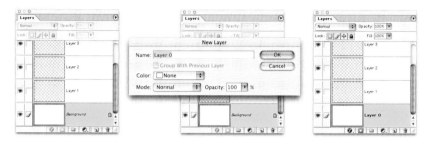

How do you apply a Layer Style to your Background layer? You can't. That is unless you double-click on your Background layer. This brings up the New Layer dialog where you can rename your Background layer, and when you do, it turns into a regular layer. Now you can apply Layer Styles to your heart's content. Want an even faster way? Just hold the Option key (PC: Alt key) and double-click, then you won't get the dialog box at all—it will just convert it into a new layer named Layer 0.

⚫ ⚫ ⚫ LOCK, LOAD, AND MOVE LAYERS

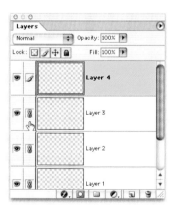

Want to move two or more layers at the same time? Link the layers together and then they'll move as one unit. To do that, go to the Layers palette and click in the second column beside all the layers that you want to move. You'll see a tiny Link icon that looks like a chain appear indicating that the layers are linked. Now you can use the Move tool and drag the current layer to a new position. As you do, all the linked layers will move also. To unlink a layer, click directly on the Link icon in the second column.

MANAGING YOUR LAYERS

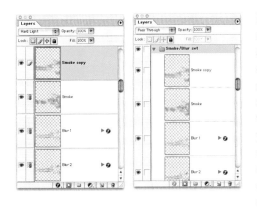

If you have lots of layers that relate to each other (for example, if you're working on a logo and have six Type layers in that logo), you can create a layer set and put all six layers in that one set. What are the advantages of a layer set? For one, you can collapse the layer set so that only the folder for the set is showing, which makes your Layer palette significantly shorter and easier to navigate. Plus, with layer sets you can delete all the layers in the set by simply dragging the set to the Trash icon, or you can duplicate the entire set by dragging the set to the New Layer icon. To create a layer set, click on the New Set icon (it looks like a folder) at the bottom of the Layers palette. To get layers into this new set, just drag-and-drop them right into your new folder. To remove them, simply drag them out to a new location in the palette.

INSTANT OPACITY CHANGE

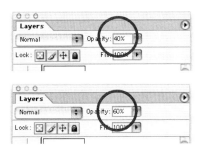

Anytime you want to change the Opacity of the layer you're currently working on, just press a number key on your keyboard: 4 = 40% Opacity, 5=50% Opacity, etc. If you want an exact percentage, such as 52%, then type in 52 (note: you have to type quickly, or you'll get 50%, then 20%).

COPY A LAYER IN THE SAME LOCATION IN ANOTHER DOCUMENT

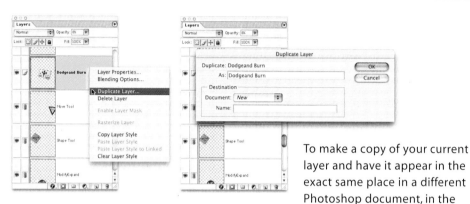

To make a copy of your current layer and have it appear in the exact same place in a different Photoshop document, in the Layers palette Control-click (PC: Right-click) on the layer you want to copy, and choose Duplicate Layer. When the Duplicate Layer dialog box appears, choose the Destination from the Document pop-up menu, and click OK.

MOVING MULTIPLE LAYERS FROM DOCUMENT TO DOCUMENT

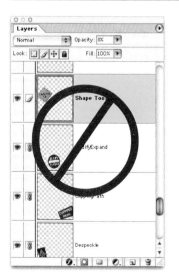

Want to move more than one layer at a time from one document to another? It's easy, as long as you know where to drag from. First, link your layers together, then make sure that you drag your layer from within your document itself, rather than trying to drag the layer from the Layers palette. Dragging a layer from the Layers palette to another document is fine, as long as all you only want to drag one layer at a time.

CENTERING DRAGGED LAYERS THE EASY WAY

When dragging a layer from one document to another, the object will appear in the new document at the point your cursor was when you released the mouse button. If you'd prefer that the layer appear perfectly centered within the other document, just hold the Shift key as you drag, and when you release the mouse button, the object will be perfectly centered.

EASIER DROP SHADOW ANGLE ADJUSTMENTS

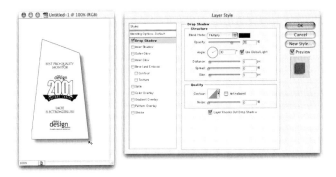

If you're creating a drop shadow using Photoshop's built-in Layer Styles, rather than setting the Distance and Angle numerically, you can adjust it visually. Just move your cursor outside the dialog box right into your image, click on the shadow itself, and drag it where you'd like it.

LAYER NAVIGATION SHORTCUT

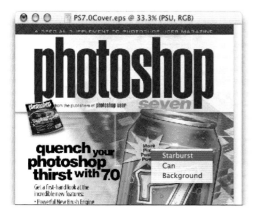

If you're working on a large, multi-layered document, you can jump to the layer you want by Control-clicking (PC: Right-clicking) over a portion of the image. A pop-up menu will appear with a list of the layers beneath the point where you clicked your cursor. To make one of those layers the active layer, just choose it from the list. It's important to note that if there aren't any layers beneath where you're Control-clicking (or the layers are transparent where you're clicking), the only layer that will appear in the pop-up menu is the Background layer.

SUPER-FAST LAYER COPIES

To instantly duplicate your current layer, just press Command-J (PC: Control-J). This also works if you want to duplicate just a portion of a layer. First, use the selection tool of your choice and make a selection of the area you want to duplicate. Now press Command-J (PC: Control-J), and that's all folks. Wait, what if you want to cut out the selected area from your current layer and put it up onto its own layer (so rather than just duplicating the layer, you're cutting it from the layer, and putting it onto another)? Then press Shift-Command-J (PC: Shift-Control-J). This works great if you want to take the contents of your Background layer and put it onto its own separate layer, without deleting the Background layer. Here's how it works: Press Command-A (PC: Control-A) to Select All, then press Shift-Command-J (PC: Shift-Control-J) to cut the background image out and put it on its own layer, above the now blank Background layer.

INSTANT LAYER ALIGNMENT

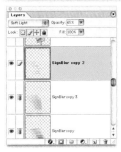

In Photoshop 6 and 7.0, aligning layers is easier than ever. Just link the layers you want to align, then choose the Move tool. In the Options Bar, you'll see icons for aligning horizontally, vertically, and to the left, right, and center, plus icons for equally distributing the spacing of your layered objects.

SEPARATION ANXIETY: PUT A LAYER STYLE ON A SEPARATE LAYER

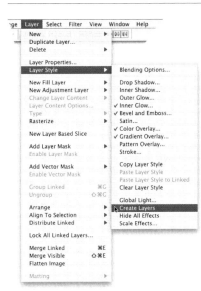

When you apply a Layer Style to a layer, you've done just that—applied a Style to a layer, and that Style is married to that layer. However, if you'd like to edit your effect separately from the layer, you can ask Photoshop to take the Layer Style and put it on its own separate layer (or layers if necessary). To do this, go under the Layer menu, under Layer Style, and choose Create Layers. Your effect will now appear on its own Layer beneath your current layer. Note: If you apply a bevel effect, it will create multiple separate layers.

LAYER EFFECTS REMOVAL SPEED TIP

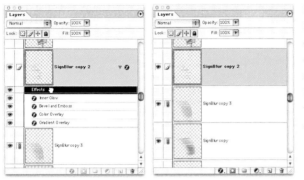

If you want to remove all the Layer Effects applied to a particular layer, don't drag them all into the trash one by one. The fastest way is to simply drag the word "Effects" right into the Trash icon at the bottom of the Layers palette, and all the effects go right along with it.

JUMP TO ANY LAYER JUST BY CLICKING IN YOUR IMAGE

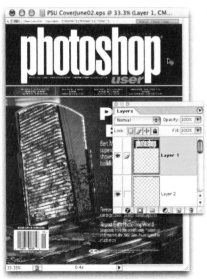

You can jump to any layer in your document without going to the Layers palette. Press "v" to choose the Move tool. Now, press the Command key (PC: Control key), and click on an object on a layer in your image that you want, and you'll instantly jump to that layer.

COLOR-CODING MADE EASY

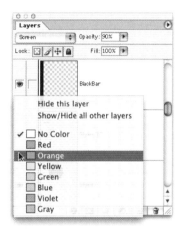

Back in Photoshop 6.0, Adobe introduced the ability to color-code layers and layer sets for quick visual identification, but to do this, you had to bring up the Layer Properties dialog and choose your colors from a pop-up menu. In 7.0 it's much faster—at least if you know this shortcut: Control-click (PC: Right-click) on the Eye icon next to the layer you want to color-code and a pop-up menu of colors will appear where you can choose the shade you'd like.

CAN'T PAINT ON A LAYER? HERE'S WHY

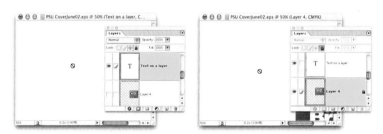

If you try and use one of Photoshop's paint tools to paint on a layer but Photoshop gives you the international symbol for "no you're not!", it's probably caused by one of two reasons: (1) You're trying to paint on a Type layer. Photoshop only allows one thing on Type layers—type! If you need to paint on a Type layer, you must first rasterize it (which converts it from an editable Type layer into a regular image layer). (2) The other reason is probably that the layer has been "locked" for painting. Look up in the top of the Layers palette and uncheck either the box that looks like a paintbrush or a padlock (which Locks All).

SPEED UP PHOTOSHOP BY MERGING LAYERS

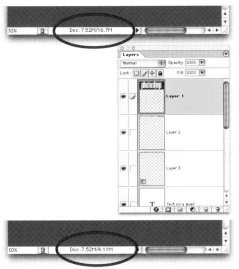

Every time you add a layer to Photoshop, it adds quite a bit of file size to your image. The larger your file size, the slower Photoshop goes. If you're creating a document that has lots of layers, before long, your file size is going to get pretty huge. One way to keep things lean and mean is to merge any layers that don't need to be separate. You do this by clicking on the topmost layer in the Layers palette, and then pressing Command-E (PC: Control-E). This merges the current layer with the layer directly beneath it. Think of it this way—every time you merge two layers, your file size drops and Photoshop gets faster. It's like a keyboard shortcut that adds more horsepower.

LAYER SET SUPER-SPEED TIP

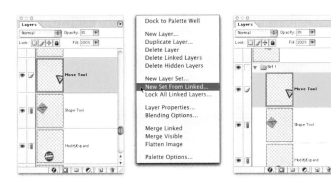

Want a quicker way to create a layer set? Link all the layers you want to include in this new set, then hold the Option key (PC: Alt key) and from the Layers palette's pop-down menu, choose New Set From Linked. This will create a brand new set consisting of all of your linked layers.

SAVE ROOM IN YOUR LAYERS PALETTE

This is a quick little tip for keeping your Layers palette shorter and more manageable. When you apply Layer Styles to your layers, each effect is listed separately in the Layers palette by default. If you apply five or six effects to one layer, it takes up a ton of room in your palette, and before you know it, you're scrolling farther and farther down the palette. To have it take up dramatically less space, collapse the effects in the palette by clicking on the down-facing triangle next to the little "*f*" icon to the right of the layer's name in the Layers palette. You can expand this list of effects anytime by clicking in the same spot.

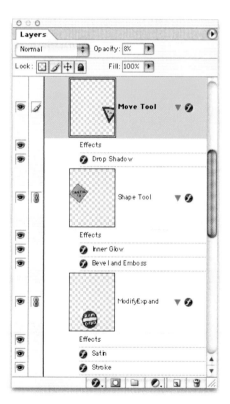
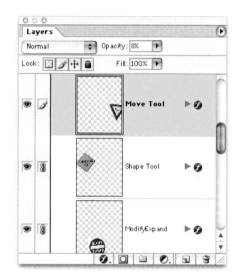

CAN'T WE ALL JUST HAVE THE SAME STYLE?

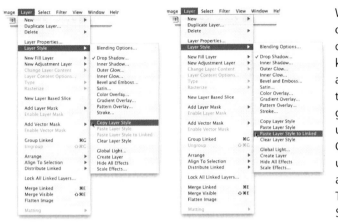

Want to apply a Style that's on one layer to a bunch of other layers? It's easy (if you know the trick). Just link all the layers that you want to have that same Style, then go under the Layer menu, under Layer Style, and choose Copy Layer Style. Then, go under that same menu again and choose Paste Layer Style To Linked, and your copied Style(s) will instantly paste to every linked layer.

LAYER PALETTE NAVIGATION SPEED TIPS

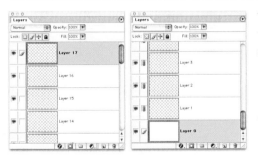

The less you need to be in the Layers palette, the better (at least when it comes to speed), so here are some shortcuts you'll want to know: To jump to the bottom layer in the palette, press Shift-Option-Left Bracket ([) (PC: Shift-Alt-Left Bracket). To jump to the top of the layer stack, press Shift-Option-Right Bracket (]) (PC: Shift-Alt-Right Bracket). To move your current layer down one layer at a time, press Command-Left Bracket (PC: Control-Left Bracket). To move it up one layer at a time, press Command-Right Bracket (PC: Control-Right Bracket). To switch to the layer beneath your current layer, press Option-Left Bracket (PC: Alt-Left Bracket). To switch to the Layer above your current layer, press Option-Right Bracket (PC: Alt-Right Bracket).

QUICK COPY YOUR LAYER MASK

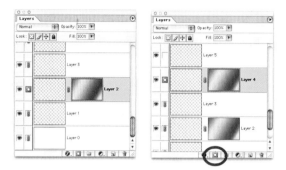

If you've applied a Layer Mask to an image, you can duplicate that Layer Mask and apply it to another layer fairly easily. Start by clicking on the layer where you want this Layer Mask to appear. Then, click directly on the Layer Mask thumbnail that you want to copy and drag it down to the Layer Mask icon at the bottom of the Layers palette. When you do this, it creates an exact copy on your new layer.

SELECT EVERYTHING ON YOUR LAYER IN ONE CLICK

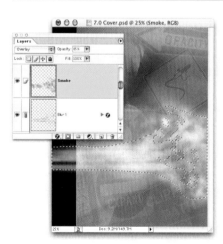

If you have a layer that contains many objects, you can put a selection around every object on that layer by holding the Command key (PC: Control key) and clicking on the Layer's name in the Layers palette. This is ideal in situations where you have an object that is heavily feathered or has a flattened drop shadow. If you use this trick, it will look like it only selects the most opaque portion of the image, but when you move it, you'll find it has selected every pixel on the layer, including the soft-edge pixels—it won't leave anything behind.

VIEW YOUR LAYER MASK AS A RUBYLITH

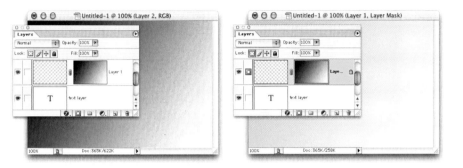

If you want to view your Layer Mask by itself (rather than how the Layer Mask affects your overall image), hold the Option key (PC: Alt key) and click directly on the Layer Mask thumbnail in the Layers palette. This will display just the Mask itself. You can also view the Layer Mask like a Rubylith (a red overlay used in traditional masking) by pressing the Backslash key (\) on your keyboard.

SELECTING JUST ONE OBJECT ON A LAYER

If you have multiple objects on the same layer (like a few words of type that have already been rasterized) and you want to select just one item on that layer (for example, you want to put a selection around one letter so you can move it independently of the rest of the letters), here's how: Use the Lasso tool to draw a very loose selection around the object. Hold the Command key (PC: Control key), and then press the Up Arrow key once and the Down Arrow key once. The entire object will become perfectly selected without disturbing anything else on the layer. Now you can move it, edit it, or tweak it separately because it is now a "floating selection."

KEEP LAYER STYLES FROM AFFECTING NEW WORK

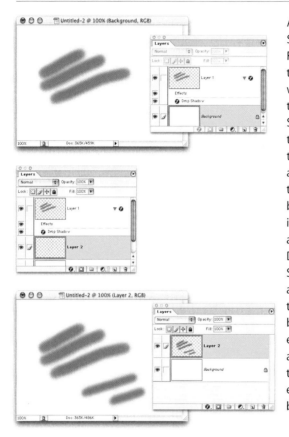

As you know, when you apply a Layer Style to a layer, it affects the entire layer. For example, if you apply a Drop Shadow to a layer, everything you do on that layer will have the same Drop Shadow applied to it. But what if you've applied a Drop Shadow and you want that shadow to remain, but you want to do other things on that layer without having an automatic drop shadow added to them? Here's what to do: Create a new blank layer by clicking on the New Layer icon at the bottom of the Layers palette, and drag this new layer beneath your Drop Shadow layer. Click on your Drop Shadow layer (to make it the active layer), and then press Command-E (PC: Control-E) to merge it with the blank layer directly beneath it. This will remove the active effect from the layer (so it no longer applies a drop shadow to new things on the layer), but it will leave the shadow effect on the objects that were there before the merge.

UN-FILLING FOR FUN AND PROFIT

In Photoshop 7.0, Adobe brought a once-buried command front and center when they added the "Fill" opacity to the Layers palette. This isn't your average everyday fill. No sir, this is a special freaky fill that only works when you've applied a Layer Style to a layer. To see it in action (and immediately understand its power), create some text, and then apply a drop shadow. Lower the regular Opacity of this layer, and you'll notice that both your type and the shadow fade at the same time. Now raise it back up to 100%. Then lower the Fill amount (in the Layers palette) and you'll notice that the type fades away, but the drop shadow stays at 100%. Ahhhhhh. Makes you stop and think, doesn't it?

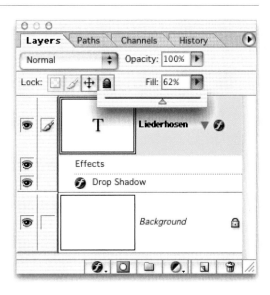

OPACITY SLIDER SPEED TIPS

If you're using the Opacity slider in the Layers palette, you can control this slider (which frankly is a bit awkward to control with your mouse) by using the Arrow keys on your keyboard. Here's how: Click on the right-facing triangle next to the Opacity field, then use the Left and Right Arrow keys to move 1% at a time. If you hold the Shift key, you'll move 10% at a clip.

CHANGE LAYER SET BLEND MODES WITH CAUTION

Be careful when you're changing the Blend Mode of a layer set (rather than just an individual layer), because the Blend Mode of the set overrides the Blend Mode of the individual layers within the set. If you click on the individual layers of the set after you change the set Blend Mode, they appear to have their original Blend Modes intact; however, you'll find that the set's Blend Mode has overridden all of the layers' Blend Modes.

AVOIDING THE LAYER MENU

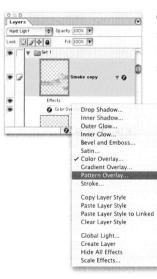

Once you've applied a Layer Style to a layer, if you need to access some related commands that are in the Layer menu, you don't need to go up to the Menu bar and go digging through the submenus. Instead, Control-click (PC: Right-click) on the little "ƒ" icon that appears to the right of your layer's name in the Layers palette. A pop-up menu will appear with most of the Layer Style menu commands right at your fingertips—without the searching and digging through menus.

MORE CONTROL OVER BLENDS: ADVANCED BLENDING

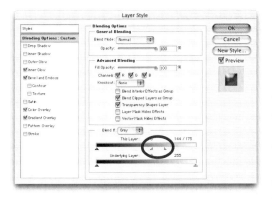

Using Blend Modes is a great way to get the layer you're on to interact with the layers beneath it. The only problem is you don't have much control over these Blend Modes—they either look the way you want them to, or not. They're pretty much an "on" or "off" tool. If you're looking for that next level of control over how layers interact with each other, you need the advanced Blending Options. These are found by double-clicking on the layer. What appears onscreen looks like the Layer Style dialog box (and in fact, it is), but if you look closely, you'll see two slider bars giving you control over how your layered images interact. Here's another quick tip: If you hold the Option key (PC: Alt key) before you drag one of the sliders, it will split the slider in two, which gives you smoother transitions and more usable blend effects.

 ## SHAPES WITHOUT THE SHAPE LAYER

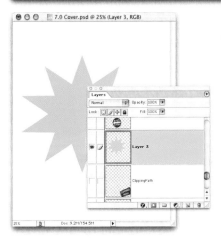

If you use Photoshop's Shapes tools, by default they create a Shape layer (which is basically a layer filled with your Foreground color, with a clipping path in the shape of your shape, if that makes any sense). We've had loads of e-mails from users asking us, "Do I have to have that funky Shape layer? Can't I just have the shape without the layer and clipping path?" Absolutely! When you choose one of the Shapes tools, look up in the Options Bar and on the far left you'll see three icons. Click on the third icon from the left and you'll get just the shape—no Shape layer, no paths, no kidding.

○ ○ ○ SECRET OPACITY SEE-THROUGH PART OF A LAYER TIP

This is a pretty wild tip—how to make just one part of a layer have a lower opacity. We know it sounds impossible, but this is totally cool. Start by making a selection on any layer of the area that you want to become transparent, while the rest of the layer remains at 100%. Then go under the Edit menu and choose Fill. When the Fill dialog box appears, from the Blend Mode pop-up menu choose Clear. Then lower the Opacity of the fill to whatever percentage you'd like, then click OK and voilà—part of your layer has opacity, while the rest remains at 100%. Majorly cool! (Note: You have to think in reverse here. Clear set to 100% Opacity will make the selected area completely transparent.) Wait, what if you decide later that you want to "Fill it back in"? Here's how: Just start making copies of your layer, and as you do, you'll see the transparency disappear. You may have to make five or more copies, but son of a gun if it doesn't work. When it looks right, hide all but those copied layers, and from the Layers palette's pop-down menu, choose Merge Visible.

I've got to be honest with you, I'm not sure you really need this chapter, so let's do a little quiz to start things off, and if for some reason you

Speed Freak
troubleshooting tips

fail this impromptu quiz, then you'll have to read the chapter. Pass, and you jump straight to Chapter 9. Ready? Begin (you have 12 minutes for the first segment).

Question One: If Photoshop crashes while copying a 50-MB file into Clipboard memory, do you (a) pack up your computer, call Billie Joe MacAllister and ask him to meet you at the Tallahatchie bridge; (b) completely disrobe, sit cross-legged on the floor while burning candles around the Photoshop product box; (c) press Shift-Alt-Control-Delete-Tilde-Tab-Escape-Enter-Option-F15-Backslash, proving you have eleven fingers; or (d) all of the above?

Answer: It was a trick question. Obviously, the real answer would have been "b," except you never, never dare to have an open flame anywhere near your Photoshop product box. Sorry, grasshopper—turn the page and start reading.

LET'S DO THE TEXT WARP AGAIN

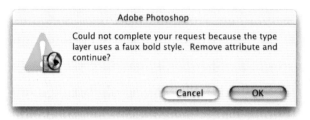

Adobe Photoshop

Could not complete your request because the type layer uses a faux bold style. Remove attribute and continue?

Cancel   OK

I get more people than you can "stick a shake at" asking me about this problem. If you go to use Photoshop's Warped Text function, you might get a warning that states, "Could not complete your request because the type layer uses a faux bold style." A faux bold style? What in the wide world of sports is that? Actually, it's a feature of Photoshop (that was introduced back in Photoshop 5.0) that lets you create a fake (faux) bold or italic type style for fonts that don't really have a bold or italic type style. It's toggled on/off in the Character palette's pop-up menu. In Photoshop 7.0, Adobe added the option in the warning dialog to "Remove attribute and continue." All you have to do is click OK to remove the faux bold and now you can Warp your text. Life is good.

UNLOCKING THE BACKGROUND LAYER

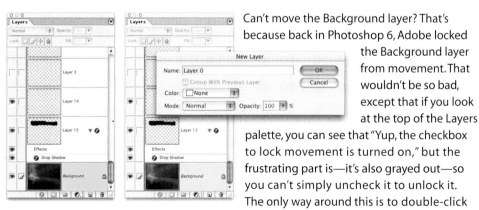

Can't move the Background layer? That's because back in Photoshop 6, Adobe locked the Background layer from movement. That wouldn't be so bad, except that if you look at the top of the Layers palette, you can see that "Yup, the checkbox to lock movement is turned on," but the frustrating part is—it's also grayed out—so you can't simply uncheck it to unlock it. The only way around this is to double-click on the Background, which brings up the New Layer dialog box. Click OK, and your Background layer becomes Layer 0 and is unlocked. Now you can move it.

TRIMMING YOUR PLUG-INS FOR FASTER STARTUP

If Photoshop takes forever to load on startup, there may be a good reason. One of the things that takes a long time to load are Photoshop's plug-ins. The more you have, the longer it takes. These plug-ins also eat up RAM, so when it comes to plug-ins, less plug-ins means faster Photoshop. One way around this is to create a custom folder of just the plug-ins that you use on a daily basis. That way, only the plug-ins you really need will load. Here's how: Simply create a new folder, and name it something like "slim plug-ins" or "Slim Whitman plug-ins" or even perhaps "hair plug-ins." Next, make a copy of just the plug-ins you want in this set and put them in your newly named folder. To make this your active plug-in set, just hold Shift-Command (PC: Shift-Control) while launching Photoshop and a dialog box will appear asking you to choose which plug-ins folder you want to use. Choose your "slim plug-ins" folder and click OK, and that set will load from now on. If you ever want the full default set of plug-ins to load instead, just hold the same keyboard command and choose "Plug-ins" as your set to load.

THE REAPPEARING/DISAPPEARING BRUSH TIP

This one gets more people because it's a feature that acts like a bug. Has this ever happened to you? You're working in Photoshop, you're using the Paintbrush tool, and everything seems fine. But a little later in your session, you get the Paintbrush tool again, and it no longer displays the size of the currently selected brush tip. Instead, it displays a little crosshair cursor. So you go to the Preferences menu and choose Display and Cursors, and sure enough, you've got "Brush Size" chosen as your preference, but for some strange reason, it's not showing your brush size; it's showing that stupid crosshair. Here's the problem: Check your Caps Lock key. It's turned on, and turning it on changes your Paintbrush cursor from displaying brush size to displaying the crosshair. This is actually a feature to be used when you need to see the precise center of your brush. The problem is it's assigned to the Caps Lock key, so every time you turn on Caps Lock when you're working with type, you just temporarily switched your Paintbrush cursor. Does Adobe need to find a better key for this feature/bug? You betcha! Will it happen? Not as far as I know.

DO YOU HAVE ENOUGH RAM? ASK PHOTOSHOP

Not sure if you have enough RAM? Just ask Photoshop. Believe it or not, it can tell you. Here's how: Open a document that's indicative of the type of image you normally work on. Work on the image, doing typical stuff, for about 10 minutes. In the bottom left-hand corner of your document window, just to the right of the current document magnification readout, is the Info box. By default, it's set to display your document's file size, but if you click-and-hold on the right-facing triangle to the right of it, a pop-up list of options will appear. Choose Efficiency. If the percentage shown is 100%, you're gold, baby! That means that Photoshop is running at peak efficiency, because 100% of the time your image manipulations are being handled in RAM. If the efficiency number shown is, say 75%, that means that 25% of the time, Photoshop ran out of RAM and had to use free hard drive space to make up for it, which means Photoshop ran *much* slower 25% of the time. An efficiency of 75% is pretty much as low as you want it to go. If it shows anything less than 75%, it's time to buy more RAM. Pronto!

HOW TO USE RGB FILTERS ON GRAYSCALE IMAGES

If you're working on grayscale images, you'll find there are some Photoshop filters that won't work (they're grayed out, so you can't access them). Of course, it's always the really cool filters, such as Lens Flare and Lighting Effects, that are grayed out. But don't be dismayed (in fact, be "mayed") because you can still use those filters—just switch to RGB mode, run the filters, then switch back to Grayscale mode. It won't affect the color of your image because, well, there is no color—you're working on a grayscale image. Switching to RGB doesn't suddenly pour color onto your image; your grayscale image will still look grayscale in RGB. When you switch back to Grayscale mode (after applying the filters), you'll get a warning asking, "Discard color information?" You can safely click OK, because after all, there was no color to begin with.

⬤ ⬤ ⬤ THE KILLER TROUBLESHOOTING TIP: DELETING THE PREFERENCES

This is probably the most important tip in this entire chapter because if something goes wrong in Photoshop, almost regardless of what it is, deleting Photoshop's preferences file will usually fix it. In fact, if you call Adobe tech support, this is usually the first thing they'll tell you to try when you're having problems, so you might as well beat them to the punch. All you have to do is find the Preferences file, delete it, then (and this is key) restart Photoshop, and the program will automatically build a new factory-fresh set of preferences, and chances are

that'll fix the problem. The only hard part of this repair scenario is actually finding the preferences themselves, which apparently were hidden by the same person who hid Jimmy Hoffa, so they're not easy to find. Here's where to look:

Windows 98:
Windows\Application Data\Adobe\Photoshop\7.0\Adobe Photoshop 7 Settings

Windows NT:
WinNT\profiles\<username>\Application Data\Adobe\Photoshop\7.0\Adobe Photoshop 7 Settings

Windows 2000:
C:\Documents and Settings\<username>\ApplicationData\AdobePhotoshop\7.0\Adobe Photoshop 7 Settings

Windows XP:
C:\Documents and Settings\<username>\ApplicationData\Adobe\Photoshop\7.0\Adobe Photoshop 7 Settings

Macintosh 9.x:
System Folder\Preferences\Adobe Photoshop 7 Settings\Adobe Photoshop 7 Prefs

Macintosh X:
Users\<username>\Library\Preferences\Adobe Photoshop 7.0 Settings\Adobe Photoshop 7.0 Prefs

GETTING BACK YOUR BACKGROUND LAYER

Lost your Background layer? It happens. It's heartbreaking, but it happens. If you suddenly find yourself staring at a Layers palette and there's no Background layer (chances are you accidentally converted your Background layer into a regular layer), here's how to get a Background layer again: Create a new blank layer. Then, go under the Layer menu, under New, and choose Background from Layer, and Photoshop will take your new blank layer and create a solid white Background layer at the bottom of your layer stack.

GETTING PRINT RESOLUTION FROM YOUR DIGITAL CAMERA IMAGES

Problem: You imported an image from your digital camera, and although the physical dimensions of the image are rather large, the resolution shows up as only 72 ppi. How can you get enough resolution to print this image? Solution: Go under the Image menu and choose Image Size. Turn off Resample Image, then in the Resolution field, type in the resolution you need for the specific device you'll be printing to. When you do this, Photoshop will automatically input the Height and Width that would result from using that resolution (the image size will definitely be smaller—the higher the resolution needed, the smaller the physical dimensions of your image). All you have to do is click OK and Photoshop will do the math, creating an image in the new smaller size, with the new higher resolution. The good news is by doing it this way, there's absolutely *no* loss of quality to the file whatsoever.

FIXING THE "ROUNDED CORNERS" SELECTION PROBLEM

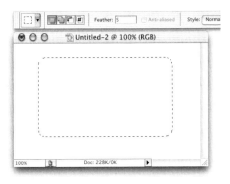

Ever have this happen? You draw a selection with the Rectangular Marquee tool (the square/rectangular selection tool) and the corners of your selection are rounded, rather than nice and straight? This happens to a lot of people, especially if they've been drinking. If you haven't been drinking but you're suffering from rounded-corner selections, look up in the Options Bar, and you'll see a field for Feather. Chances are there is some number other than "0" in this field, and what's happening is every time you draw a selection with that tool, it's automatically feathering (softening) the edge. What probably happened is you either intentionally (or accidentally) added a feather amount at some time, then later forgot to set it back to its default of zero. So to fix it, just highlight the field and type 0. Incidentally, this is a great Photoshop prank to play on coworkers, friends, soon-to-be-enemies, etc., because the Feather field is usually the last place they'll look.

MAKING GLOBAL LIGHT WORK FOR YOU

Problem: You applied a drop shadow to an object on one layer, then later, you applied a bevel on another layer, but in the Bevel and Emboss dialog box, when you go to change the angle of your bevel, you notice that the position of your drop shadow just moved as well. Reason: Adobe uses a feature (that acts like a bug) called Global Light. The idea behind it makes sense, yet we've never run into the scenario it was created for. The idea is this: You've created an image with lots of drop shadows, all casting in a particular direction. If the client saw your work and said, "Hey, instead of having the shadows go down and to the right, can we make all the shadows go up and to the left?" If that unlikely event ever occurred, you'd be set, because all you'd have to do is move one shadow and all the other shadows on other layers would move to the exact same angle. It's a great idea; it just never happens (okay, it's probably happened somewhere, once). Solution: In the Layer Style dialog box, uncheck the Use Global Light box. Now you can move the angle of your current Layer Style separately from the rest of your image. Life is good once more.

FIND THE HIDDEN MAGNETIC PEN TOOL OPTIONS

I know what you're thinking—finding the Magnetic Pen tool options? I didn't even know there was a Magnetic Pen tool in the first place. Adobe has done a great job hiding it, and in 7.0, its options are buried even deeper than before. For some reason they must hate this tool. Anyway, to get to the Magnetic Pen tool (the magnetic part means it snaps to well-defined edges to help you draw accurate paths around objects) you have to start by choosing the Freeform Pen tool from the Toolbox. Only then will the subterranean

magnetic checkbox surface in the Options Bar. However, to access the all-important "Magnetic Options" so you have a chance in hell of actually controlling this tool, you have to dig deeper into the underground world of 7.0 to make these options bubble to the top. Click on the down-facing black triangle to the right of the Custom Shape tool icon in the Options Bar to reveal a pop-down menu few will ever see—the Freeform Pen Options. In this rarely viewed menu, you'll find a checkbox for "Magnetic," and clicking on it will bring the grayed-out Magnetic options to life, and open a treasure chest of newfound riches (also known as more boring options).

PRINTING SHADOWS OVER SOLID COLORS IN PAGE-LAYOUT APPS

This is such a cool tip (I'm not sure it's a troubleshooting tip, but the concept causes so many problems, that we thought we'd stick it here). The problem is this: How do you put an object (such as a chair, a clock, or some sort of silhouetted image) with a soft drop shadow over a colored background in your page-layout application (such as QuarkXPress, InDesign, or PageMaker)? Think about it. It's harder than it sounds. You can't use a clipping path, or it will clip off the soft edges, leaving an unsightly white edge. The ideal solution is to create the entire background in Photoshop and put your object and shadow over that background, and then export the whole shebang as one giant file into your page-layout program. Unfortunately, oftentimes, because of the particular project you're working on, you simply can't do that. So how do you pull off this mini miracle? Create what's called a dithered shadow. It's not hard, but it's kind of scary for most people. Here's how:

Step One: First, go under the Image menu and make a duplicate of your object image by choosing Duplicate.
Step Two: Change your Foreground color to 40% gray, and then go to your object layer and press Shift-Option-Delete (PC: Shift-Alt-Backspace) to fill your object with gray. Apply a Gaussian Blur to make your 40% gray layer have soft edges (this will become your shadow).
Step Three: Convert your RGB image into Grayscale mode by going under the Image menu, under Mode, and choosing Grayscale. When the dialog box appears asking if you want to discard the color, click OK.
Step Four: Now convert your Grayscale image to Bitmapped mode. When the Bitmap dialog box appears, under Output enter 600 using pixels/inch and set the method to Diffusion Dither. Rename the file and save it in TIFF format.
Step Five: Import your shadow into your page-layout application, and then import your original Photoshop object (with a clipping path applied so you get just the object, not the white background surrounding it) and position it over your shadow where you'd like it (of course, be sure to position the shadow so that it extends outside your object and is clearly visible).
Step Six: This is the critical (read scary) part of this process. In your page-layout application, you *must* set this TIFF shadow to overprint the background (rather than knockout, like it normally would). This way, when you image the film at high resolution, the shadow will appear smooth and will overprint the background, looking like a soft shadow without the white halo. One reason this technique freaks people out is that onscreen, you still see the white pixels over your background in your page-layout application, so it takes a leap of faith to print something that onscreen looks wrong, but will fix itself thanks to the overprinting. It's a gutsy technique, but people pull it off everyday. Tough people. Gutsy people. Mostly Marines.

● ● ● LET PHOTOSHOP REBUILD YOUR PREFS

If you need to delete Photoshop's current
preferences file (which is a common "first-line-
of-defense" troubleshooting move), you don't
have to go digging around your drive. In 7.0,
all you have to do is hold the Shift, Option,
and Command keys (PC: Shift-Alt-Control)
when you first launch Photoshop, and you'll

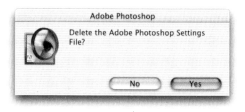

be greeted with a dialog box asking you if you want to delete the Photoshop Settings File.
If you do, click yes, and Photoshop will build a new factory fresh set of preferences for you.

● ● ● KEEPING YOUR LAYER STYLES INTACT IN ADOBE AFTER EFFECTS

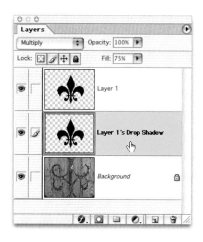

This tip is for using layered Photoshop files with After
Effects, Adobe's video effects application. A popular
technique is to take a layered Photoshop document
and animate each layer independently. The problem
comes when you apply Layer Styles in your image—
After Effects ignores them, so all your cool bevels and
drop shadows disappear. Here's how to get around the
problem: Before you save your file for importing into
After Effects, go to each layer that has a Layer Style
applied, then go under the Layer menu, under Layer
Style, and choose Create Layer. This puts the effect
(even bevels) on their own separate layer(s) beneath
your original layer. That way, the effects are still visible
when you open the file in After Effects because they're
no longer Layer Styles, they're individual layers. Better yet, you can now animate the effects
individually because they're on their own layers. If you don't want them separate from the
object they were applied to, click on the object layer, then press Command-E (PC: Control-E)
to merge the object layer with the effect layer(s) beneath it.

FASTER APPLICATION SWITCHING

Do you often copy and paste images from Photoshop into other applications (such as FileMaker Pro, Word, etc.)? I'm not talking about importing a TIFF or EPS, I'm talking about copying the object, switching to another application, and pasting your copied image from the clipboard. You don't? Great, then we have a tip for you that will speed up your application switching pretty dramatically. Go under the Photoshop menu, under Preferences, under General, and turn off the checkbox for Export Clipboard (in Windows and Mac OS 9.x, Preferences can be found under the Edit menu). Here's what's happening when it's turned on: Whatever you last copied in Photoshop gets transferred to your system's Clipboard memory when you switch to another application, just in case you want to paste. If you have a large image in clipboard, you'll get a dialog box with a status bar saying "Exporting Clipboard," and while it's there, you can only sit there and wait. Turn off that preference, and wait no more.

STOP THE CROP SNAPPING

Problem: When you're trying to crop an image using the Crop tool, your cropping border tries to snap to the edges of your document window. This might also be happening when drawing large marquee selections as well. Solution: Press Shift-Command-; (PC: Shift-Control-;), which is the shortcut for turning off this snapping. The only downside is it turns off all snapping (like snap to guides, snap to rulers, etc.). If you just want the Crop snapping (or Marquee snapping) off, go under the View menu, under Snap To, and choose Document Bounds, and your tools will no longer try and snap to your, well, document bounds.

⬤ ⬤ ⬤ THE SCOOP ON ROUNDED CORNERS WHEN EXPANDING SELECTIONS

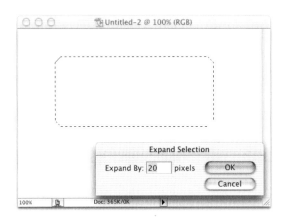

We don't have a solution to this problem, but at least you'll know you're not the cause. Here's the scoop: When you make a selection, and then want to expand the selection, you can do that by going under the Select menu, under Modify, and choosing Expand. The problem occurs when you expand more than just a couple of pixels. What happens when you expand by say five or six pixels? The straight edges of your selection become rounded. What's the fix? As far as we know, there isn't one. You're going to have rounded corners. Hey, at least you know.

⬤ ⬤ ⬤ GETTING SMALLER PHOTOSHOP FILES

Do your Photoshop .psd file sizes seem a little large? It may be because of a preference setting that makes Photoshop save a flattened version of your Photoshop image, along with your layered Photoshop file. Why does Photoshop do this? Because there's a slight possibility you might share this file with someone using Photoshop 2.5 (just like there's a slight possibility that Congress will vote to cut their own salaries), and Photoshop 2.5 didn't support layers, so it can't read your layered document. But because, by default, that flattened version is included in your layered file, guess what—2.5 can open the flattened image. What luck! Who cares? I'd rather have smaller file sizes all year long, and if you would too, go under the Photoshop menu (the Edit menu in Windows and Mac OS 9.x), under Preferences, under File Handling, and uncheck the box called "Always Maximize Compatibility for Photoshop (PSD) Files." Think about this one for a minute and you'll wonder why this is turned on by default. Think about it for two minutes and you'll wonder why it's in Photoshop at all. Don't spend too much time on it, or you'll start to wonder who's the poor soul that's stuck on version 2.5.

KEEPING YOUR JPEGS LOOKING GOOD

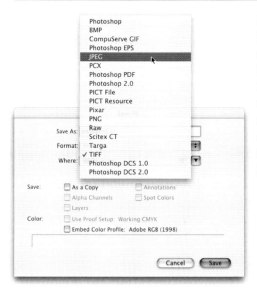

Problem: The image you saved as a JPEG looked okay in Photoshop, but after you've edited, saved the image, and reopened the image, it looks pretty bad. Solution: Don't keep resaving images as JPEGs, because each time you save an image as a JPEG, Photoshop recompresses the file, throwing away more data as it goes. Save the same image as a JPEG four or five times and you might as well drag it into the Trash (Recycle Bin).

MAKING YOUR COLOR PRINTOUTS MATCH YOUR MONITOR

Are the images that come out of your color inkjet printer looking much different from what they looked like on the screen in Photoshop? Are the images oversaturated and do they just look unnatural? There could be a host of reasons, but one of the first things to check is which color mode you're in when you're printing. The problem is this: Many people switch to CMYK mode before printing their image, because, after all, their printer has four inks: cyan, magenta, yellow, and black. The problem is you're not printing color separations, where you get four sheets from one image: one cyan, one magenta, one yellow, and one black. Instead, you're printing a composite image (one page with all the colors, rather than four separate sheets), so in most cases, you should stay in RGB mode for results that will better match your screen. Most color inkjets produce much more accurate results when you're using RGB images (the printers actually do a special RGB to CMYK conversion in the printer driver to make use of the CMYK inks, but if you do it first, all hell breaks loose). Not sure if this is true? Try a test on your printer: Print the same image twice—once in RGB mode, then convert the exact same image to CMYK and try again. In just a few seconds, you'll have the definitive answer.

GETTING BETTER EPS PREVIEWS

Problem: The image looked great in Photoshop, but when you converted it to CMYK, saved the file as a TIFF, and placed it into QuarkXPress, InDesign, PageMaker, etc., the image looked awful—way oversaturated and totally whacked. Reason: The preview of CMYK TIFFs just looks like that, so don't freak out—if it looked right in Photoshop, it should print fine. Okay, what if you saved the file as an EPS, and when you place the image into your page-layout app, the color of the image looks okay, but it's not crisp and clear, but pixelated. Reason: By default the preview embedded within EPS images is a lame 256-color preview. Solution: In the EPS

Options dialog box, under Preview, choose JPEG. That way, it sends a 24-bit, full-color preview, rather than the lame 256-color preview.

CAN YOU CREATE ALL YOUR TYPE IN PHOTOSHOP?

This isn't a problem, unless you believe the myth that creating your type in Adobe Illustrator and importing it into Photoshop as an EPS will give you clean vector type, rather than bitmapped type. This is one of those Photoshop urban myths that has been passed on from unknowing suspect to naive prepress operator for years. Here's the thing: Once you place, or open, an Illustrator EPS image in Photoshop, Photoshop rasterizes the file (which means it converts it from a smooth vector file into a pixel-based file, just like you created it in Photoshop in the first place). Save yourself the trouble and create it all in Photoshop to begin with. So, why did people create their type in Illustrator and then import it into Photoshop in the past? It's because Photoshop didn't have the advanced type control that Illustrator did. The two are pretty much on a par now, except that Illustrator can still put type on a path, and that's a reasonable use of Illustrator type.

HOW TO USE ACTIONS FROM THE WEB

Wild Type.atn

Problem: You downloaded an action from a Web site, but Photoshop doesn't seem to recognize it. How do you get it into Photoshop? Solution: First, make sure the action has the file extension .atn (which lets Photoshop know it's a Photoshop action). Go to the Actions palette and, under the palette's pop-down menu, choose Load Actions. Then, locate your action and click OK, and that action will appear under its own set in the Actions palette, where you can run it.

WILL MORE RAM MAKE PHOTOSHOP RUN FASTER?

Memory Usage
Available RAM: 506MB
Maximum Used by Photoshop: 60 ▸ % = 304MB

Problem: You added more RAM to your system and assigned more RAM to Photoshop, but it doesn't seem to run any faster. Reason: Adding RAM doesn't always make Photoshop run faster. It only works if you didn't have enough RAM to begin with. Adding RAM will only help to make your computer run as fast as it can, but it won't make your 800-MHz computer run at 801 MHz. For example, if you work on Web images, and the average image you work on is 3 MB, you only need about 15 or 20 MB assigned to Photoshop to have it run at full speed. If you've got that, and add another 256 MB of RAM, Photoshop won't run any faster, because Photoshop only needs that 15 or 20 MB that you already had. Freaky.

⬤ ⬤ ⬤ DON'T USE CROP TO FIX BARREL DISTORTION

Problem: You're trying to fix barrel distortion that appears on a photo you're editing, but using the Crop tool's Perspective feature is a guessing game. You try the crop and it doesn't look right; you have to undo it, and guess again. Solution: Don't use the Crop tool's Perspective feature, even though it was specifically designed to address barrel distortion. Use the standard Free Transform tool instead, because with it, you get a live onscreen preview as you work, so fixing the distortion takes just a few seconds.

⬤ ⬤ ⬤ STOP THE "CLICK-AND-JUMP-TO-THAT-LAYER" BLUES

Problem: All of a sudden, every time you click on a layer with the Move tool, it jumps to that layer. Solution: Somehow you turned on a feature called Auto Select Layer, which lets you make a layer active by just clicking on it with the Move tool. To turn this feature off, click on the Move tool, and up in the Options Bar, turn off the checkbox for Auto Select Layer. Besides, you never really need to turn this feature on, because you can just hold the Command key (PC: Control key) and click on any layer.

We're getting near the end of the book, and I'm growing tired. Dark figures dance across the windows like so many shadows gathering dust for the fall harvest (see,

Speed 2
image-correction and prepress tips

this is why they don't let me write chapter intros at 2:30 a.m. anymore). Originally, this chapter was going to be a catchall chapter—a place for all those tips that couldn't find a home by the end of the book, but as luck would have it, we had so many image-correction and prepress tips, they actually took over the catchall chapter by force.

Now, because we stuck these image-correction and prepress tips at the back of the book, does it mean that these tips aren't as good, aren't as important, or aren't as cool as the tips in all the other chapters? Yes, that's exactly what it means. These are the tips that just aren't worth a darn, so don't even waste your time reading them, because frankly, I'm not sure how many of them really work. Oh, I'm sure one or two do, but at this point, I'm just making stuff up.

I know there are many new users of Photoshop that will be reading this book, so I think a description of the term "prepress" is in order. "Pre," as you know, means before, and "press" is derived from the Latin word meaning "to unwrinkle one's pants with an iron." So, basically, read this chapter before you wrinkle your pants.

SAY GOOD-BYE TO GRADIENT BANDING

If you've printed an image with a gradient in it, you're probably familiar with banding (a visible line where one color ends and the next starts, like bands of color, instead of a smooth transition from one color to the next). There's a very popular tip for getting rid of banding that's very effective for high-resolution imaging. Open the image in Photoshop and go under the Filter menu, under Noise, and choose Add Noise. When the Add Noise dialog box appears, for Amount enter 2, for Distribution choose Gaussian, turn on the Monochromatic checkbox, and then click OK. You'll see a little bit of this noise when viewing the image onscreen, but when printed at high resolution, the noise disappears and hides the banding. We add noise to every gradient we create for just that reason.

SHARPENING YOUR IMAGES LIKE A PRO

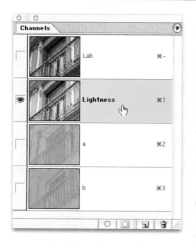

Just about every image that is brought into Photoshop, whether from a scanner, digital camera, CD-ROM, etc., needs to be sharpened. The undisputed tool for this task is Photoshop's Unsharp Mask filter. The only downside of using this filter is that to get the level of sharpening you'd like, it sometimes causes color shifts and halos, and it can also accentuate dust or specs within the image. There are two ways around this, and what's great about these methods is they let you apply a higher level of sharpening without causing color shifts or other problems: (1) Convert your file from RGB mode to Lab Color. Then go to the Channels palette and click on the Lightness channel. Now apply the Unsharp Mask filter (twice if you need it), then switch back to RGB mode (don't worry, there's no harm in this RGB to Lab to RGB mode conversion). (2) If you're working on a CMYK image, apply the Unsharp Mask filter, then go under the Edit menu and choose Fade Unsharp Mask. When the Fade dialog box appears, change the Fade Unsharp Mask Mode to Luminosity and click OK (which pretty much does the same thing as method 1, it applies the sharpening to the luminance of the image, not the color).

FIVE TIPS FOR GETTING RID OF MOIRÉ PATTERNS

If you scanned an image that already has been printed in one form or another, you're bound to get a moiré pattern over your image (moiré patterns are a series of dots or spots that appear on your image). These spots are your scanner picking up the halftone screen that was applied when the image was printed.

Here are five quick tips for removing moiré patterns:

1. Go under the Filter menu, under Noise, and choose Despeckle. There's no numbers to input or sliders to adjust—it either works or it doesn't, but luckily, it works about 75% of the time. However, if you run Despeckle and it doesn't work, undo it. That's because Despeckle adds a slight blur to your entire image, and if it doesn't work, there's no sense in leaving that blur applied, eh?

2. Apply a 1-pixel or less Gaussian Blur. This will usually work if method 1 doesn't. Again, if this technique doesn't remove the moiré pattern, undo it to reduce unnecessary blurring.

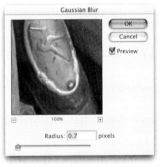

3. Go under the Filter menu, under Noise, and choose Median. Enter 1 pixel and click OK. I know I'm sounding like a broken record, but if it doesn't work, undo it. You know why.

4. Reduce the resolution of your scan to twice the line screen it will be printed at. For example, if you scanned it at 300 dpi and you're going to print it at 100 line screen, lower the resolution of the file to 200 ppi and that'll probably do the trick. If this image is going to be used on the Web, when you lower the resolution to 72 ppi, that'll probably do it.

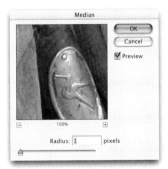

5. Lastly, try rescanning the image with the image rotated slightly on the scanner bed. This is a last resort, but if all else fails, this will probably do the trick. Once the image is in Photoshop, you'll have to straighten the scan, but at least the moiré pattern will be gone.

SCAN LINE ART AT THE RESOLUTION YOU NEED

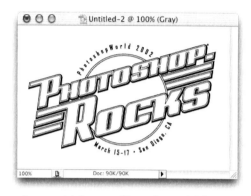

If you're scanning black-and-white line art for reproduction in print, here are two quick tips that'll help you get better results: (1) Scan the line art image at the dpi you'll be printing it. This is the one time we break our long-standing "don't-scan-at-too-high-a-resolution" rule—but only when it comes to line art. If you're going to be outputting your line art on a 600-dpi laser printer, scan it at 600 dpi. If you're going to output it to high-resolution film negs, scan it at 1,200 dpi (that's about as high as you'll need to go). (2) Scan your line art images in Grayscale mode. If you do, then you can apply filters such as the Unsharp Mask to help clean and define the lines, and you can use Levels to brighten the white areas. If you scan in Bitmap mode, you won't be able to use these two important line art cleanup tips, because they're not supported in Bitmap mode.

USING THE HIGH PASS FILTER FOR SHARPENING

There's a sharpening technique that's really gaining popularity, which works especially well on images with lots of well-defined edges (such as buildings, cars, furniture, etc.). It's actually a layer technique combined with a filter, but it's very easy (and often very effective) to apply. Start by duplicating the Background layer of the image you want to sharpen. Then, go under the Filter menu, under Other, and choose High Pass. When the High Pass dialog box appears, enter a Radius of 1.5 pixels (a good starting point) and click OK to apply the filter. It will change your image into a gray mess, but don't sweat it (yet). To bring the sharpening into your image, change the Blend Mode of this layer to Soft Light. The gray will disappear, and the edges of your image will appear sharper. You can also try the Hard Light mode to increase the sharpening effect. Still not enough? Make a copy of the layer for a multiplying effect. Is one copy not enough sharpening, but two are too much? You can control the sharpening amount in two ways: (1) Switch between Soft Light and Hard Light, or (2) lower the Opacity setting of the layer to dial in just the right amount of sharpening.

SPOT COLOR GRADIENT FILM SAVER

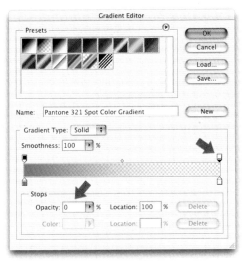

If you're creating a gradient using a spot color that fades to white, to make sure your gradient appears just on the spot separation plate, create the gradient to go from the spot color to a 0% tint of the same spot color (for example, go from red to 0% red). That way, when you do your seps, the entire gradient will appear on the red separation.

CORRECT IN CMYK OR RGB?

This is a question we've been asked a hundred times. As a general rule, we try to do as much color correction as possible in RGB mode, and if we're going to use the image on press, we only convert to CMYK at the end of the correction process. The main reason is that CMYK mode throws away data—a lot of data—and why would you want to correct an image with significantly less data than your scanner can capture? We want as much data as possible while correcting images, and when we're done, then we'll convert to CMYK and toss the data that won't be used on press.

STRAIGHTENING SCANS IN 10 SECONDS (OR LESS)

If you've scanned an image and it's crooked when you bring it into Photoshop, you can fix it in about 10 seconds flat. Just switch to the Measure tool (it lives behind the Eyedropper tool in the Toolbox) and drag it along the top edge of the image you want to straighten. That's the hard part (and that should give you an idea of how easy this technique is). Next, go under the Image menu, under Rotate Canvas, and choose Arbitrary. Photoshop automatically enters the amount of rotation (courtesy of your earlier measurement), so all you have to do is click OK and bam!—the image is perfectly straightened.

STAY AWAY FROM THE SPONGE TOOL

If you're creating images that will be output on a printing press, you're probably already familiar with gamut problems (colors that are so vivid and saturated that they're out of the range of CMYK printing). There's a tool in Photoshop that lets you paint over highly saturated areas to bring them back into gamut called the Sponge tool. Yup, it's there all right, we just don't recommend using it, because it does a somewhat harsh job of what Photoshop's going to do anyway when you convert the entire image to CMYK mode. Since Photoshop's going to do it anyway, why waste your time (and possibly mess up your image)?

REMOVING NOISE IN DIGITAL CAMERA IMAGES

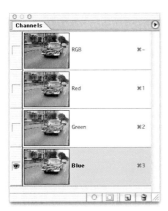

If you shoot images with a digital camera, you can almost bet that the images (when opened in Photoshop) will have some unwanted noise in the image. Most of this noise appears within just the Blue channel and knowing that, you can go to the Blue channel and add a slight blur to just that channel. This helps get rid of the noise and leaves the detail in the other channels untouched. Here's how:

1. Open your digital camera image in Photoshop.

2. Go to the Channels palette and click on the Blue channel to make it active.

3. Go under the Filter menu, under Blur, and choose Gaussian Blur. When the Gaussian Blur dialog box appears, add a slight bit of blur (we can't give you a specific value, you'll have to experiment, but start at .5 and move slowly upward using the Up Arrow key on your keyboard).

4. When the noise has pretty much disappeared, click on the RGB composite channel and continue with your regular image correction.

SCANNERS AREN'T JUST FOR FLAT OBJECTS

Even though your flatbed scanner is normally used for scanning (you guessed it) flat images, it doesn't mean you can't scan images that have more dimension (such as a watch, a ring, a yo-yo, you name it). The only problem is, scanning an image that lifts the lid adds lots of ambient light into your scan, introducing so many outside colors and reflections that it makes the scan all but unusable. The tip for getting around this is deceivingly simple: Just put a black sweater (or black felt cloth) around the object you're going to scan, and you'll get great-looking scans, even with the lid open. The black sweater soaks up that ambient light and you'll be amazed at how natural and balanced your scanned objects will look.

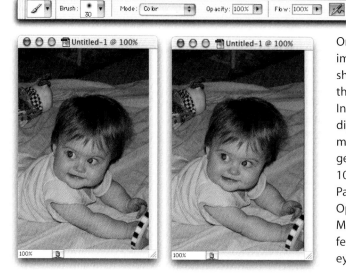

INSTANT RED-EYE REMOVAL

One of the most common image mishaps for images shot with a digital camera is the appearance of "red eye." In fact, you'd swear that most digital cameras are "red-eye machines." Here's a tip for getting rid of red eye in about 10 seconds—just get the Paintbrush tool, and in the Options Bar change the Blend Mode to Color. Now paint a few small strokes over the eye and the red eye is gone!

ARE YOUR COLORS PRESS READY?

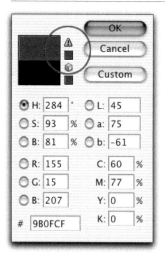

If you're working on an image that will be printed on a printing press and you select a color that is outside the range of what a CMYK press can reproduce, you'll get what's called a Gamut Warning right within Photoshop's Color Picker. This is just to let you know that the color you've chosen is outside the CMYK gamut. Just below the warning (shown at left) is a tiny Color Swatch showing you what the color you picked will really look like when printed in CMYK mode. To find out where that color resides within the Color Picker, click once directly on that tiny swatch and Photoshop will pick that color for you.

NEVER SWAP COLORS AGAIN WHEN CLEANING LINE ART

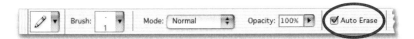

When cleaning up line art images with the Pencil tool, you can spend a lot of time going back and forth to the Toolbox to switch your Foreground color to black (to fill in missing pixels) and then to white (to erase pixels that shouldn't be there in the first place). It does help if you use the keyboard shortcuts "d" to set your Foreground to black, and then "x" to make white your Foreground color, but there's actually a faster way. Once you select the Pencil tool, go up in the Options Bar and turn on Auto Erase. What the Auto Erase option does is pretty neat—when you click the Pencil in a black area of pixels, it paints white; when you click it on a white pixel, it automatically paints black. It happens automatically—so you never have to switch colors again—saving you a ton of time, travel, and keystrokes.

LET PHOTOSHOP DO YOUR RESOLUTION MATH

You don't need a calculator to determine how much resolution you need for printing to a particular line screen—Photoshop will do all the math for you, right inside the Image Size dialog box. Here's how: Open the image you want to print. Go under the Image menu and choose Image Size. When the dialog box appears, click on the Auto button (it's right under the Cancel button). When the Auto Resolution dialog box appears, all you have to do is type in the line screen of the device you're printing to and then choose a quality setting. Here's how Photoshop does its resolution math:

Draft: This just lowers your resolution to 72 ppi (ideal for onscreen use, the Web, etc.)
Good: This takes the line screen and multiplies it by 1.5
Best: This doubles the line screen (multiplies it by 2)

When you click OK, Photoshop enters the math it just did into the Resolution field of the Image Size dialog box.

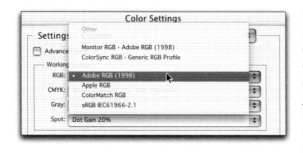

GOING TO PRESS?
MAKE SURE YOUR MONITOR IS IN THE "RIGHT SPACE"

By default, the RGB space for your monitor is set to sRGB, which is an okay mode for designing Web graphics. However, if you're producing graphics for print, the sRGB mode is just about the worst RGB space your monitor could possibly be set at. It clips off lots of colors that are actually printable in CMYK mode, and therefore is pretty unsuitable for prepress work. We recommend changing your RGB workspace to an RGB space that's more appropriate for doing print work. We like Adobe RGB (1998), which is a very popular RGB space for prepress work. You choose this RGB space under the Photoshop menu, under Color Settings (in Windows and Mac OS 9.x, Color Settings can be found under the Edit menu). When the Color Settings dialog box appears, under the Working Spaces areas, for RGB choose Adobe RGB (1998) from the pop-up list of working spaces.

WANT BETTER GRADIENTS ON PRESS? HERE'S THE TIP

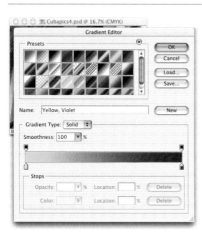

If you're designing a job that will ultimately go to a printing press in CMYK mode and it's going to contain one or more gradients, you'll get better printed results (less color shifts) if you create those gradients after you convert to CMYK mode.

GETTING BEFORE AND AFTER PREVIEWS

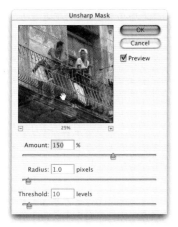

If you're applying a correction filter, such as the Unsharp Mask filter, you can get a before and after view of your image even before you click the OK button (and then pressing Command-Z [PC: Control-Z] to undo/redo the filter). Instead, click-and-hold on the preview box inside the Unsharp Mask filter. When you click-and-hold, you get the before preview in the window; when you release the mouse button, it shows you how the image will look with the filter applied. Pretty handy. If you need to see the full preview on screen, you can toggle the Preview checkbox on or off. Another tip is to hold the Command or Option (PC: Control or Alt) button while in a filter dialog box, and then your cursor changes into the Zoom tool. You can then zoom in or out in your preview window by clicking within it.

CLONING FROM IMAGE TO IMAGE

If you're retouching an image using the Clone Stamp tool, not only can you clone from the image you're in but you can also clone from any other image that you have open. All you have to do is make sure both images are open at the same time. Go to the other image, Option-click (PC: Alt-click) on the area you want to clone from, switch back to the image you're working on, and then start painting. When you do, you'll be cloning image data from the other image.

GET MORE REALISTIC DROP SHADOWS ON PRESS

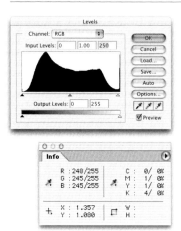

Here's a quick tip for getting more realistic drop shadows in print: Add some noise. In the Layer Style Drop Shadow dialog box, there's a slider for adding noise to your shadows. When you add just a small percentage, it makes your shadows appear more realistic when they show up in print.

MAKING SURE YOUR WHITES ARE REALLY WHITE

If you have an image that appears to have solid white areas (maybe the background surrounding a logo), but when you put the Eyedropper on that area, it gives you a 1 or 2% reading in one of the CMYK values in your Info palette, you can use Levels to gets those areas back down to 0% so they don't print with a dot. Here's how: Go under the Image menu, under Adjustments, and choose Levels. The third field from the left (at the top of the dialog box) shows your current highlight value (your white point setting). The default value will be 255. Enter 252 or 250, then move your cursor over the white area in question and look in the Info palette to see if the readings are now all 0% (that change should be enough to remove the stray colors). When it's right, click OK, and you'll have solid white in your white areas.

TRY NOT TO CORRECT MORE THAN ONCE

When correcting images in Curves, Levels, etc., it's best to try and do all your corrections at one time rather than changing each setting individually (by that I mean, don't set a highlight in Curves, then close it and reopen to set a shadow). The reason is, each time you apply a tonal correction, it puts some strain on the quality of the image. So to keep your image from having unnecessary data loss, when you open Curves or Levels, make your shadow, highlight, and midtone adjustments, and then click OK to apply all three adjustments at once.

HAVE PHOTOSHOP HELP FIND YOUR HIGHLIGHTS/SHADOWS

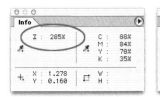

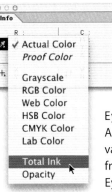

Not sure where the highlight or shadow points in your image are located? Let Photoshop help. Go under the Window menu and choose Show Info. In the RGB readout, click on the tiny Eyedropper icon to the left of the readout. A pop-up menu will appear with a list of values you can measure. Choose Total Ink from this pop-up list. Next, switch to the Eyedropper tool and move it over your image in the areas you think might be the darkest. Now, up in the Info palette, look for the highest number. When you find the area in your image with the highest number (the highest amount of total ink), you've found the shadow point. Do the same to find the highlight—just look for the lowest number. When you locate that number, you've found the highlight.

TALKIN''BOUT MY RESOLUTION

Here's a lingo tip about resolution. Although images can have a resolution from 1 to more than 2,000 ppi, when it comes to talking resolution, there are three basic resolutions that are pretty common. Low-res (short for resolution) is normally 72 ppi, and low-res images are primarily used for onscreen viewing (such as the Web, slide presentations, digital video, etc.). Medium-res is generally 150 ppi and is commonly used for printing to inkjet and laser printers. When people use the term high-res, it's almost always referring to 300 ppi, which is more than sufficient resolution for printing to a printing press. Anything above 300 ppi is still considered high-res, but you'd say it like this, "I made a 600-ppi high-res scan." Which resolution is right for you? Nice try. That's a whole book unto itself.

ARE YOU REALLY SEEING YOUR SHARPENING?

When you apply sharpening to your image using the Unsharp Mask filter, make certain that when you apply it, you're viewing the image at 100% size. Most other views won't give you an accurate view of how the sharpening is really affecting the image. To make sure you're viewing at 100%, just double-click the Zoom tool in the Toolbox.

ADJUSTING CURVE POINTS WITH PRECISION

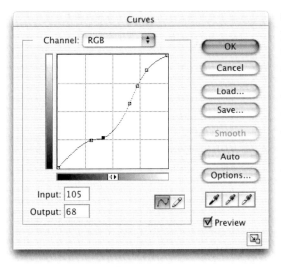

Once you've plotted a point on a curve, you can adjust these points by clicking and dragging them, but many people find it easier to plot the point by using the Up/Down Arrow keys on their keyboard. This adjusts the Output of the point in increments of 2. To adjust the Input, use the Left/Right Arrow keys. To make larger moves, hold the Shift key while using the Arrow keys and your points will move in increments of 15.

APPLY UNSHARP MASK TO CMYK IMAGES

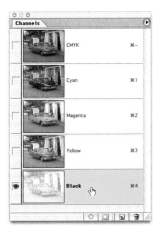

If you've already converted your image to CMYK mode and you want to quickly sharpen your image without introducing color shifts or halos, go to the Channels palette, click on just the Black channel, and apply your Unsharp Mask there. Applying the filter just to the Black channel will enable you to apply a higher level of sharpening without damaging the image.

RGB FLESH TONES: GETTING THE "RED" OUT

If you're working on an RGB image and you've done your basic color correction but the flesh tone in your image still seems too red (a common problem), here's a tip to fix it fast. First, select the flesh tone areas in your image (using the Lasso tool, etc.). Add a slight feather by going under the Select menu and choosing Feather. Enter 1-pixel feather for low-res images, 3 to 5 pixels for high-res images. Go under the Image menu, under Adjustments, and choose Hue/Saturation. From the Edit pop-up menu, choose Reds. Then lower the Saturation slider until your skin tones look more natural and click OK.

ONCE YOU'RE IN CMYK MODE, STAY THERE

You've read some techniques in this chapter that require you to be in either RGB mode or Lab Color mode; however, if for whatever reason your image is already in CMYK mode, do not (I repeat, do not) convert to RGB or Lab mode for *any* reason. Once you've converted to CMYK mode, the data loss from the conversion has already occurred, and switching back to RGB mode won't bring back those lost colors. What's worse is, if you switch from CMYK to RGB (or Lab), when you convert back to CMYK mode, you'll go through another CMYK conversion and damage your image even more. The moral of this story is—once you're in CMYK mode, stay there.

THE SIMPLE TIP TO BETTER COLOR SEPARATIONS

Converting from RGB mode to CMYK mode for printing is easy, just choose CMYK from the Mode menu under the Image menu. However, getting great-looking separations on press takes more than just choosing the CMYK menu command. Before you convert to CMYK mode, call the print shop that's printing your job and ask them for their Photoshop CMYK separation setup. They'll provide you with custom settings to input in the CMYK Setup dialog that will give you a separation that's tuned to their particular printing press. Once they provide you with those settings, you input them by going under the Photoshop menu and choosing Color Settings (in Windows and Mac OS 9.x, Color Settings can be found under the Edit menu). When the Color Settings dialog box appears, click on the CMYK pop-up menu, and at the top of the menu choose Custom CMYK. The Custom CMYK setup dialog will appear where you can enter the settings given to you by the print shop. Once entered, then you can make your CMYK conversion, and you'll get a better separation that's specially tuned to the press your job will be printed on.

HOW TO SHARPEN FLESH TONES IN CMYK

When you're sharpening CMYK images, one of the toughest areas to sharpen are the flesh tones. Oftentimes, because of the soft nature of skin, you'll need a lot of sharpening, which can introduce noise and color shifts, particularly in flesh tone areas. One tip that's often used to combat this is to apply your sharpening to only the Cyan channel in the Channels palette in images where flesh tone is the focal point of the image (such as in portraits).

HOW TO READ FOUR AREAS AT ONCE

Photoshop's Color Sampler tool lets you sample up to four different color readings from within your image at the same time. The cool thing is, anytime you have one of Photoshop's paint tools (Paintbrush, Clone Stamp, Eraser, etc.), you can instantly access the Color Sampler by holding Shift-Option (PC: Shift-Alt). Click to add a Color Sampler and the Info palette immediately pops up to show you the reading. Each time you add a Sampler, the Info palette expands to show that reading (leaving your earlier readings still visible). To delete any Sampler, press Shift-Option (PC: Shift-Alt) again and just move the cursor back over the Sampler and it will change into a pair of scissors. Click right on the Sampler in your image to delete it (hint: you have to click directly on the sampler or it won't work).

MORE CURVE POINT QUICK TIPS

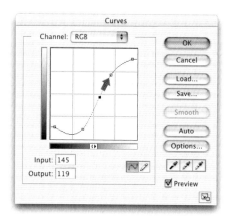

When you're working in Curves, once you've plotted a curve point, you can rotate over to the next point in your curve by pressing Control-Tab (PC: Right-click-Tab). To rotate back to the previous point, add the Shift key to make it Shift-Control-Tab (PC: Shift-Right-click-Tab). If you've got one or more points selected and want to deselect all your points, just press Command-D (PC: Control-D) to release all your points.

HEALING WITH PRESSURE

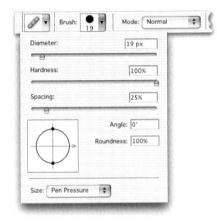

If you're using a Wacom tablet and wireless pen with Photoshop, you've probably already uncovered the secret hiding place where Adobe tucked the pressure sensitivity controls (hint: they're in the Brushes palette), but if you want to use pressure sensitivity with the Healing Brush in 7.0, it's in a totally different spot. To turn it on, click on the Healing Brush tool, then up in the Options Bar, click directly on the Brush Sample, and a menu will pop up (it's not the standard Brushes Picker). At the bottom of the menu, you'll see a pop-up for Size, where you can choose "Pen Pressure."

CONTROL THE OPACITY OF YOUR HEALING PROCESS

I don't know if you've noticed, but Photoshop 7.0's Healing Brush doesn't have an option for controlling its opacity (the way the Clone Stamp, Paintbrush, Eraser, and other tools have). But there is a workaround if you want to use the brush and have some control over its opacity. Just go ahead and use the brush

first, and then to lower the opacity of your stroke, go under the Edit menu and choose Fade Healing Brush. When the Fade dialog box appears, just lower the Opacity slider to the desired amount. It's a bit clunky, but it works.

Before you attempt any of the tips in this chapter, I have to tell you, you'll need a fairly thorough knowledge of calculus, and it wouldn't hurt

Speed Kills
advanced tips

if you kept a scientific calculator handy either. In fact, ideally, you'd put together a team with varied backgrounds and skill sets to really get anything out of this chapter. Believe it or not, that's what some people expect from an advanced tips section—tips that are very complicated and involved. But just because you're a more-advanced user, doesn't mean the tips should be harder; it just means the tips apply to more-advanced areas of Photoshop use, such as Masking, Curves, Paths, and fun stuff like that.

The tips should be easy to do, just covering more advanced topics. But if you really feel you need a complicated and involved tip to get your money's worth, here goes: Open a blank RGB document at 72 ppi. Then take a photograph of your family and tape it to the outside of your monitor. Using the Airbrush tool, choose a large soft-edged brush and draw what you see. When complete, it should look exactly like the photograph. Happy now?

POWER UP YOUR LAYER STYLES

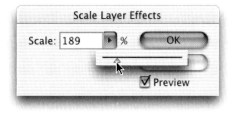

Here's a little-known tip for controlling the intensity of your Layers Styles. This is particularly helpful if you applied a number of different Layer Styles to a layer, and want to affect them all at the same time, rather than tweaking each one individually. It's called "Scale Effects," and it's buried in the Layer menu, at the bottom of the Layer Style submenu. Choose it, and a dialog box appears with a slider set to 100% by default. As you increase the amount (up to 1000% maximum), it increases the "scale" of all your effects. For example, if you increase the scale of a Layer Style drop shadow, the shadow would become blurrier and its distance from the object would become greater. If you adjusted a Stroke Layer Style, the stroke would become thicker, etc. Pretty powerful stuff.

SWAPPING FILES? MAKE SURE YOUR COLOR STAYS INTACT

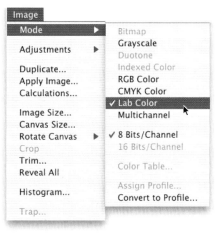

If you wind up sharing images you've created in Photoshop 7 with someone using an earlier version of Photoshop (such as Photoshop 4.0 or 5.0, which both had different color-management setups, or in the case of 4.0, didn't really have one at all), your images will almost undoubtedly look different on their monitor than the same image does on your color-managed monitor.

The trick to getting around that problem is to change the color mode of your image to Lab Color *before* you save the file you'll be giving to them. That way, they'll see your image in Lab Color mode without having your color management info embedded within the image. In short, their image will look much closer to your image.

FREEFORM / PEN TOOL QUICK SWITCH

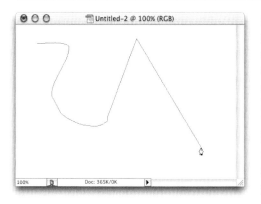

If you're using the Freeform Pen tool, there are times when you may want to temporarily switch to the regular Pen tool so you can draw a straight line segment. You can actually do this by holding the Option key (PC: Alt key) and then releasing the mouse button. This temporarily switches you to the regular Pen tool so you can draw your straight line segment by moving the mouse. When you're done, click-and-hold, release Option/Alt, and you're back to the Freeform Pen tool.

VISUAL CONTROL OVER YOUR SELECTIONS USING QUICK MASK

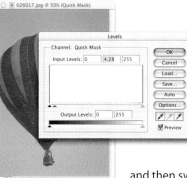

Did you know that you can use Quick Mask mode to expand or contract your selections visually? Here's how: Create a selection (using any of Photoshop's selection tools), and then switch to Quick Mask mode (press the letter "q"). Now you can go to the Levels dialog box and tweak the size of your selection. Moving the Midtone Input Levels slider to the far left makes the selected area smaller (contracting the selection). Moving the Midtone Input Levels slider to the far right makes the selected area larger (expanding the selection). The changes here usually aren't drastic, so you'd use this technique when a small adjustment to your selection is necessary, but seeing it like this beats the heck out of guessing.

CHAPTER 10 • Advanced Tips   **185**

BETTER COLOR TO GRAYSCALE USING LAB

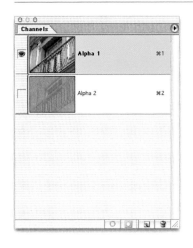

Converting a color image to grayscale by choosing Grayscale from the mode menu often produces some pretty flat-looking grayscale images. Rather than doing that, try one of our favorite tips for getting better grayscale images. Start with an RGB color scan, then go under the Image menu, under Mode, and choose Lab Color. Then go to the Channels palette. You'll see four channels. Drag the B channel to the Trash icon to delete it. Now, delete the channel called Alpha 2, leaving just Alpha 1 (which was the original Lightness channel). Now go under the Image menu, under Mode, and choose Grayscale. Go to the Layers palette and click on the Background layer. If your grayscale image appears too light, make a copy of the layer and change the Blend Mode to Multiply. If it appears too dark, lower your Multiply layer's Opacity until you dial in a perfect-looking grayscale image.

HAVE PHOTOSHOP SELECT THE SHADOWS AND HIGHLIGHTS

This is a trick we use for prepress and for photo retouching because it instantly lets you select all the shadow areas (or highlight areas if you wish) for a particular image, and it's so easy because Photoshop does all the work. To have Photoshop select just the shadow areas in your image, go under the Select menu and choose Color Range. When the dialog box appears, in the Select pop-up menu, choose Shadows and click OK. The Shadow areas are instantly selected. This is ideal for situations where your scanner has plugged up the detail in the shadow areas (pretty common in most sub-$1,000 desktop scanners). Once the shadows are selected, you can "open them up" by going to Levels and moving the Midtone Input Levels slider to the left to bring back some of the shadow detail lost in the scan.

TROUBLESHOOTING ACTIONS? SLOW DOWN!

If you're an advanced user, chances are you're no stranger to using actions, and in fact, you probably create your own (rather than using the default actions that ship with Photoshop, many of which redefine the term "useless"). If you do create your own actions, you've already found that you spend more time troubleshooting your actions than you do creating them in the first place. Well, this little tip makes the troubleshooting process a lot easier, and saves you both time and frustration. The problem is (and this won't sound like a problem) Photoshop runs actions so quickly that you don't see each step, or each dialog box, so tracking down a missing or wrong step is just about impossible. Luckily, you can actually slow down your action, or even put a pause between each step, by using Photoshop's Playback Options dialog found in the Actions palette's pop-down menu. When it appears, you can choose to play your action Step by Step, seeing everything as it happens, or you can choose to enter the number of seconds you'd like it to pause. Then, when you replay the action, you can see everything step by step and track down the culprit.

ACCESSING GRAYED-OUT FILTERS IN CMYK

One of the bad things about converting from RGB mode to CMYK mode is that many of Photoshop's coolest filters can only be applied in RGB mode, and once you're in CMYK mode, many of them are "grayed out" in the Filter menu, so they can't be accessed. So what do you do if you really want to use one of those filters? (Whatever you do, don't convert back to RGB mode, then back to CMYK. That's image suicide.) Instead, try this tip: In the Channels palette, click on the Cyan channel. Go to the Filters menu and you'll notice that all those grayed out filters are now suddenly available. All you have to do now is apply the filter you want to each channel individually (once each on Cyan, Magenta, Yellow, and finally the Black channel), and the filter will appear as though you applied it to the entire image (in reality, you did—you just did it the more laborious way). One way to speed up this process is to create an action that will do it all for you with one click of the mouse.

MORE CONTROL OVER FILTERS

We love Photoshop's Fade command (which acts like an "undo on a slider"), and when it comes to applying filters, we use it all the time to gain more control (including blending mode control) over filters we apply. The only downside to the Fade command is you can only use it one time—you get one opportunity to Fade, or choose a Blend Mode, then you're stuck. Here's a tip to keep the control of your filters for as long as you'd like: When you're about to apply a filter, make a duplicate of the layer where you're applying the filter, then apply it. This keeps the application of your filter fully editable—you can change Blend Modes as often as you like, change Opacity, add a Layer Mask to determine where the filter shows and where it doesn't, or even toss the layer in the Trash and start all over.

GETTING RID OF EDGE FRINGE WITH A SMUDGE STROKE

Earlier in the book, we showed how to deal with "edge fringe" that sometimes occurs when you select an object and put it on a different background. Our fix was to run Defringe on it (it's at the bottom of the Layer menu, under Matting). If that doesn't work, here's a more advanced tip: Start by going to the Smudge tool and choosing a very small, soft-edged brush. Then, switch to the Pen tool and draw a path around your object as close to the edge as possible (it's okay to slightly extend the path either inside or outside your edge, but don't let it extend either way more than a pixel or two). Once your path is in place, go to the Paths palette and from the palette's pop-down menu, choose Stroke Path. When the Stroke Path dialog box appears, for Tool choose Smudge and click OK. This slightly smudges the edges of your object and will often hide any edge fringe. If it smudges too much, try shrinking the size of the Smudge tool brush. If it makes the edge too soft, try a harder brush. Another "hide-the-edge fringe" trick is to Command-click (PC: Control-click) on the Layer that contains the object (in the Layers palette) to put a selection around the layer. Then, go under the Select menu, under Modify, and under Contract select 1 pixel, and click OK. Next, go under the Select menu and choose Inverse, and then press Delete (PC: Backspace) to trim 1 pixel off your object all the way around. In some cases, this works wonders.

APPLYING MULTIPLE FILTERS? NOT ON MY LAYER!

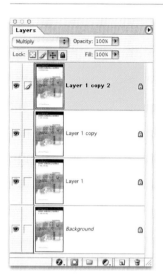

Thinking of applying a number of different filters to a particular layer? Don't do it. Instead, make a copy of your layer, then apply the first filter. Make another copy of the layer and apply the second filter; make another copy, apply the third filter, and so on. You can use Photoshop's Layer Blend Modes to get the effect that one filter is applied on top of the others, and now you've got full control over each individual filter applied. If you don't like one of the filters, just drag that layer into the Trash. Better yet, you've got Blend and Opacity control you wouldn't have by simply applying filter over filter.

NEW SNAPSHOT, THE MISTAKE INSURANCE POLICY

The great thing about Photoshop's History feature is that you can (by default) undo your last 20 steps. Perhaps even more important is that you can always return to how the image looked when you opened it, so you never really do any permanent damage (as long as the file is open). However, what if you opened an image, worked on it for a while, and it was really looking great, but about 10 minutes later, it took a turn for the worse (this happens to us more often than we'd care to admit). If you undo the last 20 steps, it may not take you back far enough to the point that you want to return to, and the only other choice is to go all the way back to where you started. Here's a tip to keep you from pulling your hair out: Anytime your image is at a stage where you think it looks pretty good, go to the History palette, and at the bottom of the palette, click on the New Snapshot button. Think of it as an insurance policy so that if things go bad, you can at least return to that spot and try again. It's not a bad idea to create a new Snapshot about every five minutes when you're working on a big project. To keep from loading up on snapshots, when you create a new one, delete one or two snapshots before it.

⚫ ⚫ ⚫ SAVING YOUR ACTIONS AS PRINTABLE TEXT FILES

Save

Save As: Actions.txt

Where: ▦Desktop

Cancel Save

This is a totally undocumented actions tip, and if you need it, it's a real lifesaver. Once you've created an action, you can actually save a text document with all the action steps so you can have a printed hard copy of your action. Here's how: In the Actions palette, click on the Action set containing the action that you want to save as a text document. Hold Option-Command (PC: Alt-Control) and from the Actions palette's pop-down menu, choose Save Actions. When the Save dialog appears, you'll notice that the three-letter file extension is .txt (indicating it's a text file) rather than .atn (which is the Photoshop action format). Click OK and you've got a text file you can open in any word processor to print out your steps.

⚫ ⚫ ⚫ 3D PRINT EFFECTS (AND WHERE TO GET THOSE GOOFY GLASSES)

For a brief time back in the 1950s, 3D movies were all the rage, but it was short-lived, probably because you had to wear those cheesy-looking 3D glasses to experience the effect. Although 3D has come a long way since then, unfortunately you still have to wear the cheesy glasses. Be that as it may, the 3D effect is starting to appear again in print ads in trendy magazines, which generally include the paper 3D glasses in the magazine. This effect can be created in Photoshop, no problem. The hardest part is finding a supplier for 3D glasses (okay, we'll help on that part too. Try 3D Glasses Direct at www.3dglasses.net). Here's a tip on how to create the 3D effect in Photoshop: Open an RGB image, then go to the Channels palette and click on the Red channel. Go under the Filter menu, under Other, and choose Offset. For Horizontal enter –5 and leave Vertical set to zero. For Undefined Areas, choose Repeat Edge Pixels, then click OK. In the Channels palette, click on the RGB channel to reveal the effect. Then, lastly, you have to determine which part you want to appear as "coming out of the image" toward the person viewing it. Switch to the History Brush, and using a soft-edged brush, paint over the area you want to "jump out" from the image. As you paint with the History Brush, you'll see your original untouched image paint back in (don't sweat it, that's what it's supposed to do). Now all you have to do is order the glasses.

CREATING REUSABLE DIAGONAL GUIDES

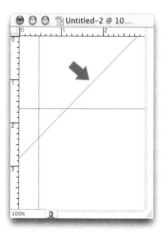

If you've used Photoshop's rulers at all, you know that you have your choice of either a vertical or horizontal guide. That's not a bad thing, but there's one thing missing—a diagonal guide. Since Photoshop doesn't have one, here's a tip for making your own: Start by creating a new layer, then set your Foreground to R=74, G=132, B=255 (the color Photoshop uses for its built-in guides). Switch to the Line tool found in the Shapes tools, and on this new layer draw a diagonal line where you want your guide to appear (make sure you have Create Filled Region selected in the Options Bar). It's not a bad idea to copy that layer into a separate document and save it on your drive—so anytime you need a diagonal line, you can just open that document and drag it right in.

FASTER SCANNING FOR MULTIPLE IMAGES

This is a handy tip when you're batch-scanning images (scanning a number of different images at once). For example, let's say that you scanned eight small images on your scanner, all in one pass. When this scan opens in Photoshop, you've got one huge image with eight little images on the page. Here's the fastest way to get those eight little images out of that one main document and into eight separate documents: Drag a Rectangular Marquee selection around one of the images, and then press this series of keyboard shortcuts: Command-C, Command-N, Return, Command-V, Command-E (on PC that would be Control-C, Control-N, Enter, Control-V, Control-E).

This copies the tiny image under your selection, opens a new document, inputs the exact size of your copied selection, pastes the copied image from the Clipboard into your new document, and then flattens the image to just a Background layer. You'll be amazed at how quickly you can press those five quick combinations and turn one big timesaving scan into eight separate images in just seconds.

SAVE TRIPS TO THE SELECT MENU

Here's a huge timesaver: When you have a selection applied to an area of your image, you can instantly access a number of commands you would most likely want to use by Control-clicking (PC: Right-clicking) within the document itself. This brings up a context-sensitive pop-up menu with a list of commands that pertain to selections, including Save Selection, Select Inverse, Feather, Fill, Stroke, and Free Transform. By using this shortcut, you can save yourself trips to the Menu bar and access some features that don't have a built-in keyboard shortcut (such as Save Selection).

DRAG-AND-DROP CURVES FOR QUICK CORRECTION

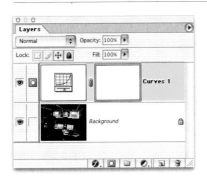

If you're color-correcting a number of images that are basically the same (for example, catalog shots or high-school yearbook shots, where the lighting and composition are pretty much the same), you may want to apply the same Curve setting to a number of images. Rather than saving the Curve setting and loading it each time, try this tip: Use a Curves Adjustment layer, and then just drag-and-drop that layer from your current image to your target image.

ACTIONS POWER TIP: ADD AN ACTION TO YOUR ACTION

Here's an Actions power tip: Did you know that you can build an action that will include an existing action? Here's how it's done: As you're recording your action, just go to the Actions palette, click on the existing action you want to include in your current action, and press the Play button at the bottom of the Actions palette. The existing action will now be added as a step in your current action (pretty scary stuff).

PREPRESS CLEANUPS—IN A SNAP

This is a great tip if you're retouching images, or checking an image in prepress for spots or specs, because it lets you check the entire image in a very methodical way—using your keyboard to navigate zone by zone. Here's how:

Press the HOME key to jump to the upper-left corner of your image window.
Press the END key to jump to the lower-right corner of your image window.
Press the PAGE UP key to scroll upward one full screen.
Press the PAGE DOWN key to scroll downward one full screen.
Press Command-PAGE UP (PC: Control-PAGE UP) to scroll one full screen to the left.
Press Command-PAGE DOWN (PC: Control-PAGE DOWN) to scroll one full screen to the right.

Once you've learned these shortcuts, you can start by pressing the Home key (jumping you to the upper left-hand corner of your image). Clean that area then press the Page Down key to move methodically down the left side of your image until you reach the bottom of your window. Then press Command-Page Up (PC: Control-Page Up) to move one screen to the right, clean that area, then press the Page Up key to move methodically up the image until you reach the top. Repeat these steps until you're finished. The advantage of doing it this way, besides the sheer speed of using keyboard shortcuts, is that you'll see every area of the image without missing a spot.

BLEND MODE POWER TIP

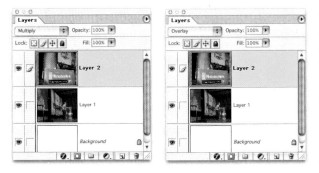

Once you understand layer Blend Modes, you wind up using them all the time. Chances are by now you know which individual modes you want to use (such as Overlay, Multiply, Soft Light, Hard Light, Screen) and which ones you'll probably never use (such as Dissolve). If you know which ones you want to use, you can use a keyboard shortcut to jump right to the Blend Mode you want. For example, to jump to the Overlay mode for a layer, press Shift-Option (PC: Shift-Alt) and the first letter of the mode you want, in this case, the letter "O" (making the shortcut Shift-Option-O [PC: Shift-Alt-O]). For Screen mode, you'd press Shift-Option-S (PC: Shift-Alt-S), and so on.

PUTTING YOUR LENS FLARE ON THE SPOT

This tip lets you precisely position the center of the Lens Flare filter by using the Info palette and a little-known feature of the Lens Flare dialog box. First, open the Info palette (found under the Window menu) then put your cursor over the precise spot in your image where you'd like the center of your Lens Flare to appear. Then look up in the Info palette, under the X and Y coordinates, and write down those two coordinates (I knew one day I'd find a use for the X and Y coordinate readings). Then go under the Filter menu, under Render, and choose Lens Flare. There's a fairly large preview window in the center of the dialog box. Hold the Option key (PC: Alt key), click once on the Preview window, and it brings up the Precise Flare Center dialog box. Enter those X and Y coordinates you wrote down earlier (you did write them down, right?), click OK, and your Lens Flare is precisely positioned.

NO MORE CREATING TYPE IN CHANNELS

If you've ever tried to create and format type in a Channel, you know what a pain it can be. Especially because, when you're working in a channel, it doesn't create an editable Type layer, so you're really limited to how you can format, and of course, edit your type. So instead of creating type in a channel (which many special channel-type effects call for), just create your type on a layer as usual. In fact, don't go to the Channels palette at all—just pretend you're not using channels. Once you've got your type formatted and adjusted just the way you want it on your regular Type layer, Command-click (PC: Control-click) on your Type layer's name in the Layers palette. This puts a selection around your type. Now you can go under the Select menu and choose Save Selection. When the dialog box appears, click OK, and it saves your perfectly formatted type as (you guessed it) a channel. Now you can delete your Type layer, and you're left with an Alpha channel with perfectly formatted type.

LET PHOTOSHOP TELL YOU THE HIGHLIGHT AND SHADOW

We use this tip to have Photoshop help us determine which are the darkest (shadow) points and which are the lightest (highlight) points in an image when we're color correcting. We start by choosing a Threshold Adjustment layer from the bottom of the Layers palette. When the Threshold dialog box appears, we drag the slider all the way to the left and the image turns completely white. We then slowly drag the slider back to the right, and the first black pixels that appear on screen are the shadow areas. We make a mental note of that area as our shadow point. Then we drag the slider all the way to the far right (the image turns black). As we drag slowly back toward the left, the first white pixels that appear are the highlight points in the image. We note them as well. We now know where the shadow and highlight points are in the image, and we can use them, along with the Eyedropper tools in the Curves dialog box, to set the proper shadow and highlight areas to remove any color casts. Note: When you've determined where the shadow and highlight areas are, you can then delete the Threshold Adjustment layer by dragging it into the Trash icon at the bottom of the Layers palette.

USING THE LASSO—DON'T STOP TO NAVIGATE

If you're using the Lasso tool, you have a surprising amount of navigation control, even while you're dragging out your selection. For example, if you're drawing a selection and you need to scroll over a bit, just press-and-hold the Spacebar, and right where your cursor is, the Hand tool will appear and you can move the image while you're still selecting (try it once and you'll see what we mean). When you let go of the Spacebar, you're right where you left off, and you can continue your selection. Here's another Lasso tip: If you're drawing a selection and reach the edge of your document window and need to scroll over, hold the Option key (PC: Alt key), let go of the mouse button, move your mouse to the edge of your image window, and you can nudge the screen over (again, this is one you have to try once to understand it). It's like you're using the Lasso tool to slide the image over. When you're done sliding, press the mouse button and release Option/Alt to continue selecting. Incidentally, while selecting, you can also use the Command- + and Command-minus zoom in/zoom out tricks (PC: Control- + and Control-minus).

LOAD ANY SAVED SELECTION WITHOUT THE CHANNELS PALETTE

If you're working on an RGB image and you've saved a selection (by drawing a selection and choosing Save Selection from the Select menu), you can instantly reload that selection at any time, without going to the Channels palette. If you only have one saved selection, just press Option-Command-4 (PC: Alt-Control-4), and the selection will instantly appear onscreen. If you have a second saved selection, press Option-Command-5 (PC: Alt-Control-5), and so on. The key to remember is that the RGB channels take up the #1, 2, and 3 spots, so always start with 4 to load your first Alpha channel. Note: If you're working with CMYK images, remember to always start with 5, because the CMYK channels take up the first four spots.

● ● ● PLOT MULTIPLE CURVE POINTS IN JUST ONE CLICK

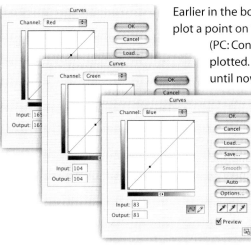

Earlier in the book, we showed you how Photoshop will plot a point on the curve for you if you Command-click (PC: Control-click) on a color in your image you want plotted. However, there's a power tip that we waited until now to share—if you add the Shift key, making it Shift-Command-click (PC: Shift-Control-click), Photoshop will add a point for that spot on all the color channels for you. This works in both RGB and CMYK modes.

● ● ● TOUGH SELECTION TIP

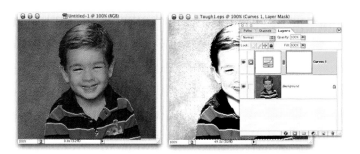

If you're struggling to make a selection of an image that is against either a background of a similar color or a very busy background, here's a masking tip to make the process easier: Add a Levels or Curves

Adjustment layer above your image layer, and use it to dramatically increase the contrast in the image to help make the edges stand out. This will often help make the difference between the object's edge and the background more obvious. The great part is, you can totally damage the look of the image because you're using an Adjustment layer. When your selection is in place, just drag the Adjustment layer into the Trash icon to delete it, and your image is back to normal, but you've got that "impossible" selection still in place.

MAKING THE COLOR PICKER SHOW CMYK

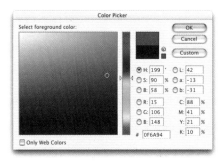

If you're working in CMYK mode and you go to the Color Picker, it still displays RGB colors. This is a bit of a problem, because you think you're picking one color, but when you start to paint or fill with that color, you get the CMYK desaturated version. Here's a tip to get around that. When you're in CMYK mode and you go to the Color Picker, press Command-Y (PC: Control-Y), which is the shortcut for Proof Colors (found under the View menu). When you do this with the Color Picker open, it changes all the colors in the Color Picker to CMYK colors. That way, when you pick a color in the Color Picker, it looks the same when you paint or fill with it in your CMYK image.

MOVING MULTIPLE CURVE POINTS AT ONCE

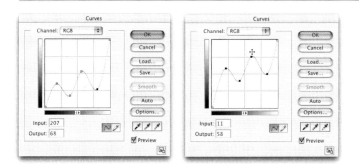

If you're working in the Curves dialog and you want to make more than one point active at the same time, click on one point (to make it active) then hold the Shift key and click on another. As long as the Shift key is held down, you can click on as many points as you'd like to make them active at the same time.

ADD TO YOUR SELECTIONS THRU THE CHANNELS PALETTE

If you've got the Channels palette open and you have multiple saved Alpha channels, you can load any Alpha channel as a selection by holding the Command key (PC: Control key) and clicking directly on the channel's name. This instantly loads the selection. An even better tip: If you hold the Command key (PC: Control key) then add the Shift key (making it Shift-Command/Shift-Control) and click on another Alpha channel, it adds that to your current selection. You can keep adding more selections to your original selection until, well… until you run out of Alpha channels.

EMBEDDING PATHS INTO ACTIONS

If you're creating actions and you want your action to include a path that you've created, you can do that, but you have to draw your path first, before you record your action. Once you've drawn your path, and it comes to the part of your action that requires the path, go to the Action palette's pop-down menu and choose Insert Path and that path will be stored along with the action.

⬤ ⬤ ⬤ MEASURE TWICE, LOOK ONCE

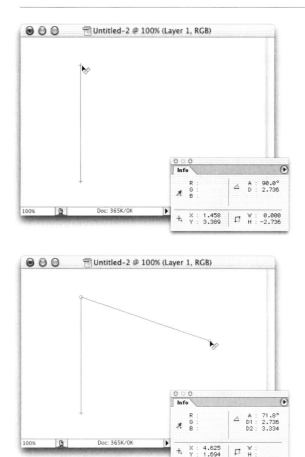

If you need to measure more than one side of an object (for example, if you're measuring a box, and you need both the height and width), you can measure both at the same time. First, open the Info palette (so you can see the measurements that the Measure tool generates), then get the Measure tool and click-and-drag it along the first edge. Release the mouse when you reach the end of the edge. Then hold the Option key (PC: Alt key), click on the end of the first line, and continue on in a different direction. You'll notice that another measurement line appears. Now, look up in the Info palette and you'll see your two measurements listed under D1 and D2.

⬤ ⬤ ⬤ STROKING HALF A PATH—HALF A PATH????

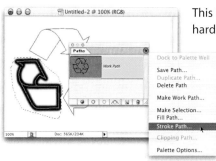

This is a mind-blowing advanced tip (not because it's hard—it's simple—but if you use the Pen tool, warning—your mind is about to spontaneously combust). Here's the scoop: If you're an advanced user, you already know that you can draw a path and then apply a stroke along that path (using the paint tool of your choice) by choosing Stroke Path from the Paths palette's pop-down menu. But dig this: If you draw your path, but only want to stroke a portion of that path, all you have to do is make a selection (using the Lasso tool) of the part of the path you want stroked. Then when you choose Stroke Path, it will only stroke the area of your path that is contained within your selection. Boom! That was the sound of our heads exploding.

⬤ ⬤ ⬤ SPEEDING UP BATCH ACTIONS

If you're running a Batch action on a folder full of images, one of the things that can really slow the process down is the fact that the History palette keeps creating History States (undos) for each image. To keep your Batch actions running at full speed, there are two things you can do: In the History palette's pop-down menu, under History Options, turn off the checkbox for "Automatically Create First Snapshot." Secondly, go under the Photoshop menu, under Preferences, and choose General (in Windows and Mac OS 9.x, Preferences can be found under the Edit menu). In the History States field, lower the number from 20 (the default) to 2 states and click OK, then your batch will run like a greased pig. Don't forget to increase your History States or change your History Options back after you're done batching or you'll be down to two undos.

⬤ ⬤ ⬤   **PHOTOSHOP WEB DESIGN HEAVEN**

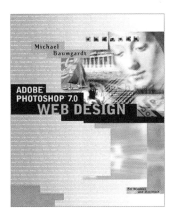

These next pages contain some of the best tips in this book, because they're tips on where to learn more about Photoshop. If you're into Web design, Michael Baumgardt's book, *Adobe Photoshop 7.0 Web Design* (Adobe Press; ISBN: 0321115619; $40.00), is outstanding, and just about the best Web Design book out there.

⬤ ⬤ ⬤   **LEARN PHOTOSHOP FROM THE GROUND UP**

If you really want to get an understanding of how Photoshop works, including the underlying principles of how it all relates, I don't think there's a better book than *Adobe Photoshop 7.0 Studio Techniques* from Ben Willmore (Adobe Press; ISBN: 0321115635; $45.00). Ben is a great teacher and he makes complex techniques very understandable. I can't recommend his book enough for anyone who really wants to learn Photoshop from the ground up.

THE BIBLE OF COLOR CORRECTION

If you're going to do some serious color correction, sometime ago Dan Margulis wrote the manual for color correction and the Photoshop community is better for it. *Professional Photoshop 6: The Classic Guide to Color Correction* (John Wiley & Sons; ISBN: 0471403997; $64.99) is a serious book—this is not a book for wusses, and honestly, the further you're along in your Photoshop skills, the more you'll get out of it. But if you've reached that point where you're ready to dive into some serious prepress, there is no other book like it.

THE INDISPENSABLE REFERENCE

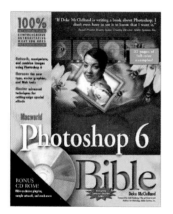

Another book you've got to have on your bookshelf is Deke McClelland's *Macworld Photoshop 6 Bible* (Hungry Minds, Inc.; ISBN: 0764534904; $49.99). It's not really one of those sit-down-and-read, cover-to-cover books, as it's over 900 pages and is so thick it can be used as a weapon. It's more of an encyclopedic Photoshop reference book, but the great thing about it is, if you have a question about a particular technique in Photoshop, you can be absolutely sure it's in this book. I've always said of Deke, "He knows things about Photoshop that Adobe doesn't even know." You'll use this book again, and again, and again. Note: Deke also has a Windows version of this book entitled *Photoshop 6 for Windows Bible.* Deke covers all the bases.

PHOTOSHOP SITES THAT ROCK: DESIGNS BY MARK

These two pages of tips are on the hottest public Photoshop Web sites. Now, because of the nature of the Web, I can't guarantee that these sites (which have all been up and running for some time now) will still be at these addresses by the time you read this book (such is the Web), but chances are, most if not all will be there, or very easy to find through a search. The first is Designs By Mark (www.designsbymark.com) which is run by Mark Monciardini, a Photoshop and graphics guru, and his site contains some great Photoshop tutorials, as well as step-by-step tutorials on Flash and Illustrator. Great stuff here, and you'll find yourself going back again and again.

THE BEST TUTORIALS ON THE PLANET

The second site tip is Planet Photoshop (www.planetphotoshop.com). I helped launch this site, and it's the only site I know of that features daily Photoshop tutorials, columns, and reviews, five days a week. I often contribute to the site with Photoshop tips or tutorials, and you'll find some very popular gurus on the site, such as Peter Bauer, Sherry London, Carla Rose, Al Ward, Josh Spivey, among others. They also post daily Photoshop-related news, and there are active discussion boards, as well.

TAKE ONE FOR THE TEAM

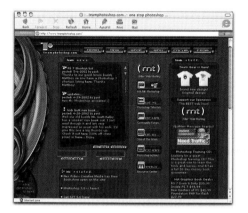

Team Photoshop (www.teamphotoshop.com) is a beautifully designed site, with loads of Photoshop info, tutorials, Photoshop Q&A, and much more. Even if you don't like Photoshop, the site is so well designed it's worth a visit, but I think you'll find you'll bookmark it (save it as a Favorite) after just one visit.

LEARNING FROM THE MOTHERSHIP

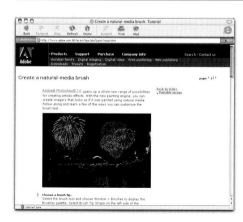

Lastly, Adobe posts lots of great tutorials (including ones from Russell Brown, Julieanne Kost, and Deke McClelland) on its site, and you should definitely check it out. Just to keep you from digging for it, the last time I looked, it was at www.adobe.com/products/tips photoshop.html, but ya' never know when Adobe might move 'em to a new location in its site, so if you lose track of them, go to the Adobe site, to the Photoshop section, and you'll find a link there.

INDEX

        www.photoshopkillertips.com

COLOPHON

The book was produced by the authors and their design team using all Macintosh computers, including a Power Mac G4 450-MHz, a Power Mac G4 500-MHz, a Power Mac G4 Dual Processor 500-MHz, a Power Mac G4 733-MHz, a Power Mac G4 933-MHz, and an iMac. We use Radius and Apple Studio Display monitors.

Page layout was done using Adobe PageMaker 6.5 and Adobe InDesign 2.0. Scanning was done primarily on a UMAX PowerLook 1100 FireWire scanner. Our graphics server is a Power Mac G3, with a 60-GB LaCie external drive, and we burn our CDs to a TDK veloCD 24X CD-RW.

The headers for each technique are set in Adobe MyriadMM_565 SB 600 NO at 9.5 on 13 leading, with the Horizontal Scaling set to 95%. Body copy is set using Adobe MyriadMM_400 RG 600 NO at 9.5 points on 13 leading, with the Horizontal Scaling set to 95%.

Screen captures were made with Snapz Pro X and were placed and sized within Adobe PageMaker 6.5. The book was output at 150 line screen, and all in-house printing was done using a Xerox Phaser 850 DX.

PHOTOGRAPHY

Kalebra Kelby, *Dave Moser*, *Felix Nelson*, *Jim Patterson*, *Rick Tracewell*, *Chris Main*, *Larry Becker*, *Ronni O'Neil*, *Jim Workman*, *PhotoDisc* (www.photodisc.com), *Digital Vision* (www.digitalvisiononline.com)

ILLUSTRATION

Scott Kelby
Felix Nelson

ADDITIONAL PHOTOSHOP RESOURCES

National Association of Photoshop Professionals (NAPP)
The industry trade association for Adobe® Photoshop® users and the world's leading resource for Photoshop training, education, and news.

http://www.photoshopuser.com

KW Computer Training Videos
Scott Kelby is featured in a series of more than 18 Photoshop training videos, each on a particular Photoshop topic, available from KW Computer Training. Visit the Web site or call 813-433-5000 for orders or more information.

http://www.photoshopvideos.com

PlanetPhotoshop.com
"The Ultimate Photoshop Site" features Photoshop news, tutorials, reviews, and articles posted daily. The site also contains the Web's most up-to-date resource on other Photoshop-related Web sites and information.

http://www.planetphotoshop.com

Photoshop Down & Dirty Tricks
Scott is also author of the best-selling book *Photoshop 7 Down & Dirty Tricks,* and the book's companion Web site has all the info on the book, which is available at bookstores around the country.

http://www.downanddirtytricks.com

Adobe Photoshop Seminar Tour
See Scott live at the Adobe Photoshop Seminar Tour, the nation's most popular Photoshop seminars. For upcoming tour dates and class schedules, visit the tour Web site.

http://www.photoshopseminars.com

Mac Design Magazine
"The Graphics Magazine for Macintosh Users" is a tutorial-based print magazine with how-to columns on Photoshop, Illustrator, QuarkXPress, Dreamweaver, GoLive, Flash, and more. It's also packed with tips, tricks, and shortcuts for your favorite graphics applications.

http://www.macdesignonline.com

PhotoshopWorld
The convention for Adobe Photoshop users has now become the largest Photoshop-only event in the world. Scott Kelby is technical chair and education director for the event, as well as one of the instructors.

http://www.photoshopworld.com

Photoshop Photo-Retouching Secrets
Scott is also the author of *Photoshop Photo-Retouching Secrets*. The book's companion Web site has all the info on the book and features downloadable source files for many of the projects. The book is available at bookstores around the country.

http://www.photoretouchingsecrets.com

Photoshop Hall of Fame
Created to honor and recognize those individuals whose contributions to the art and business of Adobe Photoshop have had a major impact on the application or the Photoshop community itself.

http://www.photoshophalloffame.com

VISIT OUR WEB SITE

WWW.NEWRIDERS.COM

On our Web site you'll find information about our other books, authors, tables of contents, indexes, and book errata. You will also find information about book registration and how to purchase our books.

EMAIL US

Contact us at this address: **nrfeedback@newriders.com**

- If you have comments or questions about this book
- To report errors that you have found in this book
- If you have a book proposal to submit or are interested in writing for New Riders
- If you would like to have an author kit sent to you
- If you are an expert in a computer topic or technology and are interested in being a technical editor who reviews manuscripts for technical accuracy
- To find a distributor in your area, please contact our international department at this address. **nrmedia@newriders.com**

- For instructors from educational institutions who want to preview New Riders books for classroom use. Email should include your name, title, school, department, address, phone number, office days/hours, text in use, and enrollment, along with your request for desk/examination copies and/or additional information.
- For members of the media who are interested in reviewing copies of New Riders books. Send your name, mailing address, and email address, along with the name of the publication or Web site you work for.

BULK PURCHASES/CORPORATE SALES

The publisher offers discounts on this book when ordered in quantity for bulk purchases and special sales. For sales within the U.S., please contact: Corporate and Government Sales (800) 382-3419 or **corpsales@pearsontechgroup.com**. Outside of the U.S., please contact: International Sales (317) 581-3793 or **international@pearsontechgroup.com**.

WRITE TO US

New Riders Publishing
201 W. 103rd St.
Indianapolis, IN 46290-1097.

CALL US

Toll-free (800) 571-5840 + 9 + 7477
If outside U.S. (317) 581-3500. Ask for New Riders.

FAX US

(317) 581-4663

WWW.NEWRIDERS.COM

VIEW CART 🛒 | search ⊙

▸ Registration already a member? Log in. ▸ Book Registration

OUR AUTHORS

PRESS ROOM

| web development | design | photoshop | new media | 3-D | server technologies |

EDUCATORS

ABOUT US

CONTACT US

You already know that New Riders brings you the **Voices That Matter**.
But what does that mean? It means that New Riders brings you the
voices that challenge your assumptions, take your talents to the next
level, or simply help you better understand the complex technical world
we're all navigating.

Visit **www.newriders.com** to find:

- ▶ Discounts on specific book purchases
- ▶ Never before published chapters
- ▶ Sample chapters and excerpts
- ▶ Author bios and interviews
- ▶ Contests and enter-to-wins
- ▶ Up-to-date industry event information
- ▶ Book reviews
- ▶ Special offers from our friends and partners
- ▶ Info on how to join our User Group program
- ▶ Ways to have your voice heard

New
Riders

WWW.NEWRIDERS.COM

PHOTOSHOP® 7

Inside Photoshop 7
Gary Bouton, Robert
Stanley, J. Scott Hamlin,
Daniel Will-Harris,
Mara Nathanson
0735712417
$49.99

**Photoshop 7
Down & Dirty Tricks**
Scott Kelby
0735712379
$39.99

Photoshop 7 Magic
Sherry London,
Rhoda Grossman
0735712646
$45.00

Photoshop 7 Artistry
Barry Haynes,
Wendy Crumpler
0735712409
$55.00

**Photoshop Studio with
Bert Monroy**
Bert Monroy
0735712468
$45.00

**Photoshop Restoration
and Retouching**
Katrin Eisemann
0789723182
$49.99

**Photoshop Type Effects
Visual Encyclopedia**
Roger Pring
0735711909
$45.00

**Creative Thinking in
Photoshop**
Sharon Steuer
0735711224
$45.00

New Riders

VOICES
THAT MATTER™